Bygone Days:
Fondly Remembered

Editor and Compiler J. Thomas Hetrick
Cover Design Pauline Kapoor

Pocol Press
Clifton, VA

POCOL PRESS

Published in the United States of America
by Pocol Press.
6023 Pocol Drive
Clifton, VA 20124
pocolpress.com

Publisher's Cataloguing-in-Publication

Bygone days : fondly remembered / editor and compiler
J. Thomas Hetrick. – 1st ed.
p. cm – (The genealogy anthology project)
ISBN: 978-1-929763-02-3

    1.   Genealogy. 2. Family life. I. Hetrick, J.
Thomas, 1957-

CS47.B94 2000   929.2'0973

Cover photograph:
Dressed in their Sunday best. Annie Blackman pushing Ron and Slyvia
in the perambulator, with Beryl carrying a bunch of flowers. Richings
Park, Iver, Bucks, England, 1931.

Table of Contents

The Genealogy Anthology Project

These stories celebrate the extraordinary lives of ordinary people. Many have departed this earth. Others are fortunately still with us. Inside are tales of survivors, of determined individuals with indomitable wills, of unfortunate children, of searchers, of story tellers, of family men, of the anguished, and of the fiercely proud. These special people live together, break bread at mealtime, worship their gods, marry, raise families, grow old, and pass away. When their immediate kin and friends also enter that great beyond, often these stories are lost forever.

The Genealogy Anthology Project (GAP) attempts, in some small way, to rectify these losses. The Genealogy Anthology Project is a series of ongoing writings intended for publication in book form by Pocol Press. Our main focus is on family narratives. In essence, this material serves as a culmination of painstaking hours spent researching, compiling, interviewing, and recording information about loved ones. There are few guidelines. Contributors can submit narratives of any length or topic, as long as they conform to the basic goal of celebrating ordinary lives. The famous or nearly-famous need not apply. We urge your participation.

Bygone Days: Fondly Remembered represents Volume One in the series.

"Where are all the joys of yesterday?"

-Peter Hammill

Robert B. Respress and his second wife, Julia.

A Father's Undying Love:
The Search for his Children
J. Thomas Hetrick

In October 1994, Jim Respress, an audio-visual specialist, shared a family reunion with three half-sisters whom he had never met.

"There are always chapters in life that are open-ended," says Jim.

The story begins five years before Jim was born. At the height of the Depression, Jim's father, Robert Respress, lived in the Fort McHenry section of Baltimore with his wife and their three daughters, aged three to five years. An athletically-built steelworker, Robert struggled to put bread on the table for his family, but the scarcity of work forced him to travel to where the jobs were, sometimes as far as Philadelphia.

This arrangement often allowed him to return home only on weekends, which became an increasing strain on his marriage. When Robert's wife could no longer deal with the situation, the couple broke up. A month after the divorce, Robert paid a visit his former Baltimore home, only to find the dwelling empty. Taking the three daughters with her, his ex-wife had vanished without a trace. Increasingly frantic, Robert canvassed his neighbors and relatives as to the whereabouts of his three daughters. No one had answers.

By 1940, Robert had moved to Virginia and re-married, eventually fathering Jim, his three brothers, and a sister, but the disappearance of his three daughters continued to haunt Robert. He would spend entire Sundays alone, driving to Baltimore and Annapolis, where several relatives lived. The Sunday drives confused the children in his new family, but whenever any of them asked questions, their mother changed the subject. Meanwhile, Robert's daughters were only vaguely aware of their sudden displacement from Baltimore, and their mother had forbidden them to make contact with their father.

Although the years passed in Robert's household, his Sunday odysseys continued. Of Robert's four sons, only Jim became curious about his dad's weekly jaunts. As a teenager, Jim approached his father about the travels on several occasions, but each time Jim's questions were evaded.

Years later, Robert operated his own construction business. After a damaging hurricane ripped through parts of southern Virginia, Robert summoned Jim from graduate school at Michigan State to help with all the new jobs. Over the summer of 1968, Jim spent a month working side-by-side with his dad.

"This was the first time I had ever had a chance to really find out what kind of a man my father was," Jim says.

After long hours of discussions, his father opened up, telling Jim the reasons behind his desperate meanderings. It was the first time that Robert Respress had ever revealed himself to any of his children. Concerned about his father's story, Jim decided to do some investigation himself. He talked to relatives and pored over phone books for clues but, like his father, Jim always reached dead ends.

In the mid-1970's and at the age of seventy-five, Robert was forced to retire from the construction business following a fall from a four-story building. His investigations, however, had finally led to the discovery that his first family had left Baltimore with a man who had been in the Navy. From there, they had traveled extensively, living in Virginia, California, and Hawaii, where his daughters survived the 1941 attack on Pearl Harbor. Robert also learned why his investigations had been so fruitless: his ex-wife and daughters had officially changed their names.

Robert died in 1978, largely as a result of his injuries, having devoted over forty years searching for his daughters.

"Every day must have been a torture for him," muses Jim. "He was forever looking into crowds of strangers, comparing facial features and wondering. Ironically, two of his daughters lived nearby. One spent fifteen years in Mount Vernon, and another lived in Annandale, Virginia."

Unknown to him, Robert's daughters were also actively involved in trying to locate him, though their efforts were continually stymied. After their mother died in 1990, however, their search intensified. Fourteen years after his death, one of the girls found a copy of Robert's 1978 obituary. Filled with misspellings and outdated information, the notice did not include the girls' names as survivors, but there was mention of Jim, then a faculty member at the University of Arkansas. During the Christmas of 1992, Jim's sister received an unusual card from a Margie Weiler in Phoenix, Arizona, and within days, there was a flurry of euphoric phone calls among Virginia, Arizona, and California. Jim had finally found his missing siblings.

After two years of trepidation, hand-wringing, and delays, the long-hoped-for meeting between Jim and his newly found sisters took place. Nine family members met in Phoenix to discover each other for the first time. Present from the east coast were Jim, his sister, and his middle brother. Greeting the party out west was sister Margie and her husband Gene. The California contingent was represented by sister Doris and her husband Frank and sister Peggy. The visit lasted four glorious days.

"We'd start early around the kitchen table and keep adding people and it would be 10:30. Then we'd say 'what are we going to do'?"

The meetings eventually moved to the back porch and onward to shopping and restaurants. Much of the talk revolved around Robert. The gatherings were full of emotion, sharing old photographs, and memories. The group spent long periods discussing their parents' motivation and their relatives' silence. The husbands of Jim's half-sisters were extremely supportive.

His sisters told of how they thought they had been abandoned. Having been brought up by their mother to believe that their father no longer cared for them, the girls were aghast when Jim told them Robert had spent years searching. In the bitterest of ironies, it developed that one relative in Annapolis had known of the girls' locations all along, yet never divulged the information to Robert.

Jim could not help noticing the similar character traits that each of his "new" siblings possesses.

"I see my dad's mannerisms in each of them. It was like I had known these people all my life," Jim recalls.

One feeling shared by all the Respress kin was the eerie but welcome spiritual presence of their father, as if he were there sharing the pain, frustration, and joy with all of them.

"It was a moment he had looked forward to all of his life," recalls Jim wistfully.

The family meetings continue. Jim's son Jeff visited Doris and Peggy while in California on an internship this summer.

"We now talk on a regular basis," says Jim, "and keep up with each other. We plan an eastern reunion soon. Two of my brothers have yet to meet the three sisters. This time the meeting will involve a special memorial service for Robert with all of his children present."

The experience has deeply moved Jim, who still has a number of unanswered questions.

Of one thing Jim is sure about his courageous father: "He sees what's going on . . . and someplace he's happy."

Reprint Courtesy of The MITRE Corporation.

"There are secrets in all families."
-George Farquhar

The family group: John Herschel Ewing, Willie Oron, Nanny
Cordelia Pirtle Ewing, Lillian Faye (circa 1910)

Hymn
CarolSue Hair

It was hot that summer of 1925--hot in a way experienced only by those who live in that part of Texas along the Red River border with southern Oklahoma. The heat was an oppressive blanket smothering the land, and even the grasshoppers were somnolent, only deigning to give desultory hops toward shadier realms when the sun struck their retreats. The super-heated air carried with it a heavy burden of humidity, so that even the slightest effort extracted its toll, and hard labor could kill a strong man. It was hot on the Ewing farm near Bowie, Texas, and the baby was sick--very sick. And so the story begins.

This is *not* a story of a Ewing family who embarked on some great journey nor engaged in wondrous adventures; nor is it a story of the exploits of Ewing heroes in conventional warfare; it is not, indeed, a tale much known in the annals of our common Ewing history. It is, instead, the account of one Ewing family, its strength, its struggles in the throes of adversity, its courage, and--most of all--its love. And it is the story of one Ewing man--son and husband and father and grandfather-- whose character and valor were an embodiment of the Ewing motto "Audaciter" as surely as if he'd engaged hordes of fierce warriors on a battlefield long ago in our ancestral Scotland.

John Herschel Ewing farmed his land and raised his family in Montague County, Texas, close to the community of Bowie. He was my grandfather. He married Nannie Cordelia Pirtle, and those Pirtle women must have held a deep fascination for the Ewing men, since Herschel's youngest brother Homer chose to marry Nannie's younger sister, Ella Pirtle.

Herschel and Nannie no doubt considered their family of six children a *fait accompli* when they discovered that my mother, Dorothy Lee, was on the way. Nannie didn't regard this as the most welcome of news, since their youngest child, my Uncle JC Ewing who has so graciously shared his memoirs and a generous amount of oral history with me, was six at this time and Nannie had entered her forties. My Uncle Oron, the eldest, was nineteen. Nannie expressed her dismay to Herschel, it is said, and he just grinned at her and exclaimed, "Why, Nannie! We need a baby around here."

John Herschel Ewing loved babies, and he adored all of his children. He was a handsome man with the most optimistic of outlooks

15

on life, a winning way with people, and a great many talents. His beautiful singing voice was heard not only at church, where he was a faithful member, but also at "singing conventions" held near and far. He was a true Christian, but neither dour nor fanatic. He delighted in inviting his own minister for Sunday dinner, along with the preachers of other denominations who had churches nearby and instigating some vigorous "doctrinal discussions" among them. He looked at life and found it good, and he shared his enthusiasm for it with his family. At this time, the family group included Irene Samantha Williams Ewing, widow of Gustavus Henry Ewing and mother of Herschel.

He had always held and expressed to all one abiding aspiration for his children--that they would each receive a full education. He knew the lack of that, and he desired that they never feel that deficit. According to my Aunt Elma Ewing Graben, all of Herschel's children were exposed early and often to the joys of good books, including but not limited to the Bible, and reading aloud from great works of literature was a regular evening ritual.

My Uncle Oron was the first to make it through high school, taking what further education was then required and becoming a teacher. It ultimately would be Oron who would see to it that his father's dream became reality, taking the task upon himself to provide an education for each of Herschel Ewing's children. All of his brothers and sisters knew the monumental sacrifices involved in this, and, not surprisingly, most of them became educators, too.

In the sweltering heat of that summer of 1925, however, the totality of my grandfather's optimism, his many talents, his sense of fun, and his ambitions for his children could not change the fact that baby Dorothy Lee was very ill, and no one knew what was wrong with her.

Herschel and Nannie made numerous trips to the doctor and to the hospital, carrying the ailing child, hoping for a diagnosis so she could begin to recover. The doctors were puzzled, the symptoms were strange, and they had to admit that they were stymied. In the meantime, the infant poured out the heat of her fever into the already scorching late-summer air.

Soon, Oron, the eldest, became ill, and the doctors then knew the answer. Oron had typhoid fever, and now it was apparent that my mother, Dorothy Lee, suffered from the same. It was current medical theory that the very young did not contract the disease, but obviously theory did not match fact--not in this case.

Typhoid fever was a scourge which came each summer to plague all of the places in our vast country where the temperature rose and the well water was untreated. It was an impartial disease, incubating its microbes randomly wherever the conditions were right. It was a killer in far too many cases, but medical science was taking the first steps toward eradicating the dreadful contagion with injections of typhoid vaccine.

When it was known that members of the Ewing family had typhoid, the ill were quarantined, and those still well were given the injections. For some of them, it worked; for others the immunization came too late. After Oron, Vernon Terrell became ill. Then Elma, followed by Georgia. Finally, exhausted from worry about his children and the labor of helping to nurse them while trying to provide for the basic needs of his family, Herschel was struck down.

This left two children, JC and Faye, and my Grandmother Nannie, along with Great-Grandmother Irene, to care for the sick and also sustain the healthy. Irene handled the cooking, while Nannie and Faye did the housework and the nursing. The health department mandated that all waste had to be buried in the ground and covered with slaked lime. JC as the youngest drew this unpleasant, but necessary, duty.

In the words of JC,, who was a very young and very frightened observer of the relentless and destructive course of the disease, "During the fall and early winter of 1925, the typhoid continued to run its course. One after another my brothers and sisters reached the critical stage of the disease, and one after the other came through the crisis. Finally, by late December, we were pretty confident that my five gaunt, emaciated brothers and sisters would indeed survive. My father, however, did not improve. Worn out by the stress of the ordeal, his strength so drained from worry, even with the knowledge that his family would survive, he was unable to fight back when his crisis came."

It was on the third of January, 1926, when my grandfather died. He was forty-three years old. He had succeeded in holding on long enough to see his children, who had been in such peril, out of their sickbeds, albeit almost too weak to walk. Herschel was aware that his time was short, and he also knew what a tremendous ordeal his death would be for the family who already had suffered so greatly. He could not prevent his departure, but he could leave his beloved wife, his mother, and his children with a final gift.

He called each member of his family to him, excepting my mother Dorothy Lee who was far too young to understand what was happening. To each he spoke the words of comfort and love that each most needed. Then he asked that they gather round him, and in his beautiful voice, which had given pleasure to so many over the years, he began to sing. The hymn he chose was "The Old Rugged Cross" and before he could complete the verses, he closed his eyes for the last time on this world. I can imagine--almost hear--the words left unsung echoing, beautiful and resonant as those to which he'd given voice, in the hushed air and in the souls of the loved ones surrounding him. He had given his all to bring his children through crisis. And in his final moments, he had bestowed on the family he held so dear the gifts of peace and comfort, the example of his courage in the face of death, and his abounding love. These gifts were theirs to keep throughout their lives and to pass on to their children. They did.

"I swear to you there are divine things more beautiful that words can tell."
-Walt Whitman

Emma: How Long is Life?
Don Wright

The hardest part of researching is watching a life unfold in front of you and then seeing it dissolve before it really starts. You see it only on paper. Emma..., you know not what she looked like; the color nor the length of her hair. Was she a slender or a plump little girl? Did she have a big smile with bright eyes? Was she happy and full of life?

Over the years you form a picture of what you think she would look like. As you continue your search, you see this little life blossom in front of you and faint pictures begin to form in your mind. Emma has been on my mind many times. Every time I find a family with young children, I wonder if the fate of these children would be like Emma's. Sometimes, I find myself wanting to close the books on research to keep from seeing these lives so shortened.

Emma was born in 1853, the fourth child of John Wright and Ruth Drake. She had two older brothers; John J. (b. 1847), and Henry Myron (b. 1850), and an older sister named Catherine, born in 1851. Unlike her brothers and sister, Emma was raised without a real mother. Ruth Drake had died two days after Emma's birth. Emma would be the only child without any memory of her birth mother. Her father John Wright, brought Christiania, his new wife into the home when Emma was only two months old.

Emma, along with her sister and brothers, were raised for their first few years with the help of her Aunt Eliza, her mother's younger sister, who had lived with them for a period of time. The children also spent many hours with their grandparents Jesse and Jemima Drake's farm. I can picture Emma, John, Henry, and Catherine running carefree on the farm just outside of town. This world would come crashing down for all four children during the next few years.

In 1856, Emma's Aunt Eliza passed away and Christiania became, not a loving mother as expected, but a woman to fear. None of the children seemed to get along with their step-mother. Young John spent as much time as he could on his grandfather's farm with his Uncle William. Seven-year old Henry ran away from home for the first time. In August 1857, Emma's stepmother gave birth to Isaac, who then kept her very busy. What normally would be a happy time in a home, may have had a devastating effect on Emma. To make matters worse, Emma's older sister Catharine, her best friend and companion, had taken sick and passed away in 1858. No doubt Emma, crushed by Catherine's death, was spending more and more time on the farm with her grandparents. Within a year of the death of Catharine, Emma's stepmother gave birth to a daughter. Surprisingly, the couple named the new baby Catherine. Would naming a child after her late sister be a torment for Emma or would it be a joy?

By 1860, young John was permanently living on his grandparents ranch in the home of his Uncle William Drake. It is possible that Henry was living there also as he was now being called by his middle name Myron. The reason for this was that another of Myron's uncles was named Henry Drake. The elder Henry Drake wasn't much older than the ten-year old boy.

In 1861, Emma's father John, with his new growing family, had moved to Marshall County, Illinois, leaving John with his grandparents. Emma also remained, which may have been at her own request.

Emma was like many young girls her age; she idolized her oldest brother John. Later that year after the Civil War had broken out, her Uncle Henry Drake enlisted in the military, and even though John was only 14, he also took up the cause. At the age of eleven, Myron (Henry) left home again, having run off to Kansas, leaving Emma as the only remaining member of the family. John was a drummer boy and in April 1862, he died at Shiloh, one of the major disasters of the Civil War. John's death may have been the last straw for the nine year-old Emma. Her father enlisted shortly afterwards and he too went off to war. Emma would never see her father again. By December of that year she was no more, passing away of unknown causes just before Christmas. In her brief lifetime, Emma had survived the deaths of her mother, her Aunt Eliza, her sister Catherine, and her brother John. To sadden and confuse her more, Emma witnessed the cruelty of her stepmother Christiania, her brother John moving away, her brother Myron running away, and a step-sister being named after her deceased sister.

Emma was laid to rest beside her sister in the Drake Family Plot, in Summit-View Cemetery, Ottawa, Illinois. Her headstone reads:

EMMA
Dau of
Mr Wright
Died
Dec 21, 1862.

Emma's is a plain inexpensive headstone as is Catherine's, about three inches thick, 18 inches wide and about 30 inches high. Both stones are side by side. Both stones have a crack through their centers, possibly a symbol of the little girls' broken hearts. The top half of the headstones has been broken off and then cemented back on. Because the name "Mr Wright" was used on the headstone instead of "John Wright," there is an assumption that John Wright had nothing to do with Emma's burial. Possibly, John Wright had gone to the small town of Henry in Marshall County, and left her with her grandparents, the Drakes, when he moved or enlisted in the military. Emma's father had been hospitalized in the military from October 1862 through 19 January 1863, which accounts for John Wright not being present at the time of his daughter Emma's death.

The sad, truncated life of Emma Wright (1853-1862) should not be forgotten.

Author note: This article was researched using notes made from my trips to Illinois, documents provided by Judy McMichaels, from stories told to me by my father Carl Wright, and from an in-depth interview with my Uncle Hartley Wright of Michigan. Both Carl and Hartley were grandsons of Henry Myron Wright and spent many years listening to his stories.

"All happy families resemble one another, but each unhappy family is unhappy in its own way.
-Leo Tolstoy

The Caseby Family: Back row, left to right, Cyril MacFarlane, George Grant, Alexander Angus. Front row, Ronald Rodger, Margaret Smith Raitt, Rev. Alexander Caseby, Williamina Caseby, Charles John. February 1943.

Food, Glorious Food
Ronald Caseby

In 1994, Rachel, my daughter-in-law, told me by telephone that her class at school was preparing an exhibition about the conditions children lived in during World War II. I still had my last ration book from 1954 and so I sent it to her as a teaching aid with her 8- and 9-year-old pupils at Thame (where the river Thames rises which flows through London), Oxfordshire.

The fact that so little confectionery was allowed (about two ounces per week) amazed her young students who consumed about two pounds weight on average per week some 40 years later. This raised a spate of questions about food and diets in general, which I attempted to satisfy with the following notes.

I think that we six healthy and fast-growing children living at The Manse, Newmills, were more fortunate than most, for my late father used all his agricultural skills to grow and store a profusion of vegetables, salad greens, and fruits to bulk up the meager protein rations of milk, meat, fish, eggs, butter, and cheese, and other essentials such as sugar and flour.

We were not keen on sweet foods and so most of our sugar rations were exchanged with the Howie family for their cheese allowance. We enjoyed cheese moulds where corn flour was cooked with it to bulk it out. This concoction was also served with salads or as a filling with cress for fresh bridge rolls. As I write I can smell the delicious Marmite covered toast topped with bubbling grilled cheese which was an alternative as the hard rind of the cheese could be used for this treat. If the cheese was maggoty then grilling it as a "Welsh rarebit" or grating it as a topping for a warming winter main course of Macaroni Cheese was another way to capitalize on the added protein. My parents, like everyone else, could not afford to waste any food during wartime.

Mr. Howie owned the "flea pit" called "The Kinema" cinema. There we children could have an enjoyable and magical Saturday afternoon watching films of "goodies," such as Tom Mix or Roy Rogers, riding the range and beating the "baddies." All this for the price of a jam jar entrance fee which was used to help the war effort. Afterwards I would gallop home, whacking my bottom with my hand as my horsewhip, with my brother Charlie for our favourite high tea of the week. We would stop our gallop home at "Batty" Makin's bakery. There we would happily wait for his rolls, "Curly Kate" tall bread loaves, flaky pastry bridies, minced beef and lamb pies, savoury sausage rolls, treacle scones, huge round sticky ginger biscuits and fruit slices to come straight from his Dutch oven on his long handled wooden "shovel." All the while we would savour the cooking smells. Then, with a basket loaded with some of these goodies, and some times with a home-made Steak and Kidney pie he had "fired" for Sunday lunch, Charlie and I would trot home at full speed to enjoy our weekly feast of good things for tea as one big happy family. Sometimes "Batty" gave us coconut tasting biscuits with red cherries on top as a treat to chew on the way home, "for being good boys," as he would say.

"Batty" Makin had been a sailor and would tell us tales of the sea when I went with one of my brothers or Bobby Talbot, to help in his bakery by pressing out pie cases or cutting out scones. He always had a hand rolled cigarette in his mouth as he kneaded the dough for the bread. He rolled his cigarettes using only one hand like the "baddie" cowboys did (the "goodies" never smoked in those days) and this skill impressed my young mind greatly. With secretive chuckling we would watch as the ash on his "fag" grew longer and eventually fell into the bread dough. Later at home it was considered to be very good luck to have a slice of his bread with a length of his ash still recognizable.

At the end of each day's work "Batty" would have a collection of odds-and-ends mixtures and contents in jars and cans from the day's baking on his working surface. Wanting to waste nothing he would chop and mix with molasses (which I think came from farmers who were supposed to use it in the making of silage for their over-wintering cattle), liquid egg, spices, lots of dried currants, sultanas, raisins and re-hydrated dried apple rings. All this would be used as the filling for his "fruit slices," which were one of my favourites. My dad said that lots of dead flies also went into them, but he like me loved the fruit slices.

Our milk supply came from "Geordie" Hedrick's farm at the top of the village, near the border with Valleyfield. Every other day I would accompany one of my older brothers to collect the milk in a quart metal container with a tight lid. What fun it was for me to watch the cows being milked, to see the hot milk running through the sieves, filters, and coolers and into the white enameled milk pails. What sheer delight it was to be given a glass of fresh buttermilk. What comfort it was to enjoy some of the thick cream from the top of the milk can on a bowl of porridge before going to bed on a cold winter's evening!

Once, being entrusted to collect the milk on my own, just after seeing a Carmen Miranda film in which a conjuror swung a pail of water over his head in a circular motion without spilling a drop, I decided to try this trick with the milk and drenched myself, as my resolution

24

wavered when the churn swung directly overhead! I went crying to Mrs. Hedrick and told her what had happened and said I would be spanked when I got home and so she cleaned me up as best she could and replenished the milk. As it was a hot summer's evening, it was not long before my cheesy smell was noted at home, my stupidity was soon discovered and I went to bed with a well "slippered" bottom that night. Dad always had to do the spanking when we were naughty, but Mum was the one who decided the punishment and saw that it was carried out. As you may have guessed, dad always used the sole of his "baffie" (slipper) because he said our thick hides hurt his hand and so he would feel more pain that we boys would.

In hot or thundery weather the milk would go "off" quickly, even in the cool larder. So, nothing ever being wasted in our household, there would be lovely hot girdle scones or Scottish thick pancakes for tea, sometimes with fruit in them. They were mouth-wateringly good when munched hot and with a little butter plus lots of home-made strawberry, raspberry, plum or rhubarb and ginger jam on them.

At school in Torryburn the third-of-a-pint milk bottles with their collectible round cardboard tops would arrive early in the morning and be frozen solid. Then the teachers would heat the crates by the big stove in the central hall and so we would enjoy a warm drink with our "leave piece" at about 10:15 a.m. In an attempt to experiment with nourishing everyone better during wartime, the Ministry of Food seemed to use Torryburn school pupils as guinea-pigs for some of its nutritional tests. For example, I recall having daily white colored Crook's Cod Liver Emulsion, malt with and without fish oil, foul tasting concentrated orange juice and, worst of all, milk tablets. These rancid smelling square milk tablets replaced our daily fresh liquid supply for a time and seemed to be made from dried milk, chalk and vitamins flavored with either vanilla, orange, raspberry, strawberry, peppermint, or almond. All were revolting, especially the almond, which put me off marzipan for life! Few pupils would eat this "confection." Many were violently sick after their first bite. Regardless, because records were being kept as part of the test, we had to accept the tablets, say we were not hungry and promise to eat them later. Then we threw them into the sea on our way home after school for the fish to enjoy. After about six months of this deception by most students in our school the experiment came to an end and our liquid milk deliveries restarted.

My "leave piece" which I mentioned earlier was always a large round "Batty" Makin white bread roll (called a bap) filled with something tasty such as butter and strawberry jam, scrambled dried egg or salad mixture, taken in a thick brown paper bag to keep it clean. I would sit on this parcel from start of lessons until our first break time when this warm flattened delicacy went down very well with the school milk. Many children would not drink milk for their parents could not afford it at home and so they were suspicious of it, therefore I often had two or three one-third-pint bottles, otherwise it would be wasted.

Occasionally a pig's head would come from the butcher and this led to frenzied activity in the kitchen. I would watch with gruesome fascination as this head with its large ears sticking out from the stock it would boil away in the jelly pan on the big black kitchen range. As I write I can still imagine the pig's bulging eyes sadly staring at me for the indignity being done to it. Then the messy and macabre ritual would continue as my mother would strip everything edible from the skull including the gray brains. She would chop it all finely so that nothing could be recognized and put it into small jelly moulds. These were then filled to the brim with the further rendered down and seasoned juices.

The moulds would set overnight into rubbery, glutinous and translucent shapes. These tasted very peppery when they were served up cold with salad things, or hot with vegetables. I always had to shut my eyes and swallow hard when I ate my "potted heid" pig's brawn. I hated every mouthful but knew that Mum was doing her best to feed us on the small stipend Dad had then as a missionary of about 130 pounds sterling per year. Fortunately, Mum always made many jars of chutney of every description and the stronger ones, such as apple or beet root and onion, green tomato, or mustard pickled vegetables, could be spread over, or eaten with, the "heid" to disguise it and kill its flavour and odour. To my young mind, one pig's head seemed to make enough moulds to last for weeks and no sooner was one finished than another would turn up. How curious, I used to think, eating a pig's head that finished up shaped like a raspberry jelly, because the moulds used were the same ones as were used to make fruit jellies for a party!

The pig's head brawn may have been off-putting as well as nutritious like the "soused" herring. Sometimes herrings were plentiful and cheap from the fishmonger's van and a large quantity would be bought. I would cover my eyes with my hands and squint through my fingers in horror as my mother would clean the entrails out of the fish and chop off their fins and heads. The cats, Trixy, Cora, An, and Nation, would have the heads and Dad would bury the "guts" in a trench under a fruit tree in the garden as a "valuable fertilizer."

The remaining fish would be rolled up, each tied together with precious string, arranged in rows in a deep dish, covered with vinegar and chopped shallots and then baked gently in the slow oven of the open coal-fired kitchen grate. This dish kept well in the larder and was then usually was served cold with salad on a Sunday lunch time and for me it was another excuse for eating more than my fair share of chutneys or pickles to disguise the taste!

Food parcels came to us from Texas, America, which were covered in thick cloth and stitched with string and their arrival brought much joy, luxury to our diet, and activity in the kitchen. These much welcomed but all too occasional parcels contained goods like tins of Spam, corned beef, pineapple and condensed milk, milk powder, chunky bars of confectionery chocolate, peanut butter, packets of cake frosting or pancake mixes. Also included in colorful illustrated packaging were fruit jelly crystals, powders to make fizzy drinks, desiccated coconut, marzipan, a slab of solid fruit cake and a big lump of what looked like coal. The "coal" was in fact dehydrated beef. Sometimes there was also a selection of dried fruits such as plums, figs, dates, bananas and grapes, chopped nuts, and several small packets of fruity tasting "polo-mint"-shaped sweets call "Life Savers" or "Refreshers."

There was always an enclosed letter from the sender and although appreciative thank you letters were sent I cannot recall any resulting correspondence. Sometimes there were fat and colorful comics used in the wrapping by the thoughtful donor and these were avidly read and exchanged amongst all the children in the village.

The parcel's cloth covering and securing strings were carefully recovered, cleaned and used for other purposes, such as boiling "clootie" dumplings, which were a must for birthdays and all festive occasions. What fun that was for the gooey liquid soap had to be bailed out of the copper boiler in the outside wash-house, then the giant copper had to be removed and swilled clean. Next it was half-filled with water and a fire started in the grate underneath. Then the precious and carefully saved flour, beef suet, spices, treacle and sugar together with the dried fruits, condensed milk and egg powder that came in the food parcel, were mixed together with an enormous wooden spoon in a great bowl and all we children were allowed to have a final stir, and taste, before making a secret wish. Finally, silver 3 shilling pieces wrapped in greaseproof paper were added and then the glutinous mixture was put into the cloth (or "clootie") tied with string to make a round shape. It was then suspended by string hanging around the clothes posser in the bubbling copper. There it boiled for about two hours making delightful smells all the while. What joy to have a steaming slice with custard, to chew the tasty outside thick skin and to be lucky enough to find a silver 3 shilling piece into the bargain. Father, always the joker, was usually the first to find a 2/6d piece in his portion and it was years before I discovered it was "one he had prepared earlier" and produced by sleight of hand.

Dad would pretend he had swallowed something and was choking. Then after a last mighty cough he contrived to have coin appear from his right ear! This find always set me to polishing off every delicious morsel in the hope of having similar luck! There was always enough dumpling left for another meal when it was fried in bacon fat to become all crispy on the outside and took on a whole new flavor and taste on the inside.

There were also treats to be made for birthdays from the other parcel "goodies." There were sweets like prettily-decorated sponge cakes with butter icing, fairy cakes, coconut ice, peppermint lumps, condensed milk hard vanilla tablet, fruity fudge, toffee apples, nutty toffee, puff candy, fruit and nut chocolate crunches. Also molded were marzipan and fudge slabs which were reshaped into small fruits. These were realistically painted with food dyes. Other treats included dates and fruit slices enrobed in chocolate, chewy Turkish delight and fizzy drinks such as American Cream Soda.

The dried egg powder was made into runny scrambled eggs. The Spam was mashed with boiled potatoes to extend it. Both of these concoctions used with lettuce to fill bridge rolls, or to be piled on small toast portions in different shapes cut out with pastry cutters and made to look attractive with slices of radish. There were colorful arrangements of cooked vegetables galantined in aspic crystals which made an exciting and filling centerpiece to any party table.

Never to be forgotten in my memories were the tasteless wobbly rabbit-shaped thick gritty chocolate custard molds surrounded by chopped green grass jelly, which had a harsh citric acid aftertaste. Lastly, but by no means least, I remember the magical bowls of trifle made from successive layers of sponge cake fingers, diced pineapple, different colored jellies, yellow custard, some sort of cream made from whipped condensed milk and topped with hundreds-and-thousands. No party was complete without its trifle.

Other treats came from the seashore where we could collect winkles and whelks, boil then in a can, and fish out the delicious morsels with a safety pin. The same pin with a raw winkle on it and attached to a long bit of string could catch a small crab from amongst the rocks at high tide and it made a tasty snack when boiled. Wild duck's eggs were also sometimes available and, although they tasted very fishy when fried on an old shovel, they were a challenge to our self-catering skills.

I was taught how to fish and cook by my four older brothers and by the gypsies who often camped near the village tennis courts, by the Quoits green at the east end of Newmills village. Our Romany friends also invited us out to try other delicacies such as hedgehogs, rabbit, or conger eels covered in clay and baked with big potatoes in the ashes of an open fire. The potatoes I willingly tried, but nice as the other foods smelled I could never bring myself to try them.

My friend, Bobby Talbot, had a mother who was a super cook and never better than when she was making potato chips in beef fat or sausage sandwiches with lots of onions and mustard in them. I always wished to taste her cooking because of the tempting smells but was never invited to join Bobby for tea with his younger brother Jimmy.

When the circus came to town, Jimmy, hand-in-hand and safe with his big brother Bobby, went to sit on the front wall of the Cooperative Society at the foot of the steep hill west of the village center. I was not allowed to join in this parade excitement as we had distant relatives visiting us that day and my presence and that of all the family was required for the special high-tea we were all to enjoy.

Bobby's and Jimmy's purpose was to watch the fairground equipment vans struggle up the steep slippery cobbled hill when wedges had to be continually shifted forwards as the heavy loads proceeded upwards. Unfortunately, one of the men slipped and did not place a restraint in time and the van rolled swiftly back to crush Jimmy instantly to death -- still holding Bobby's hand.

The Talbot family was housed in very cramped accommodation and so Jimmy was laid out for the family and friends to visit in the living room at the front of the Manse, next to Dad's study and adjoining my bedroom and that of two of my brothers. This was the first time I really had to face death and I could not grasp why the naturally happy, bright and lively and ever-smiling Jimmy was so still and white.

After the funeral I was often asked in for tea and I imagine that for Mrs. Talbot I was taking her loved Jimmy's place. In those days the local Roadman would carve various notches on the curb stones to show where there had been accidents and to tell of their seriousness. I suppose this was a timely warning to pedestrians and was constantly used by parents to instruct children on road safety. I wonder if there is still a death notch for Jimmy outside that red sandstone-faced shop at the foot of the once stone-cobbled Newmills "brae."

All the above food "events" took place in The Manse, Newmills, in England.
First appeared in RootsWeb.

"*Food come first, then morals.*
-Bertholt Brecht

Nonny and Rusty Fischer

Porch Swing Cocktails
Rusty Fischer

This is not one of those, "When Grandma was alive she used to..." stories you often read. No, my grandmother is alive and well and kicking at eighty-four and so, I guess you could call this one of those, "Let's see if MY memory is as good as hers" type of stories...

My grandmother baby-sat for me every Saturday night when I was growing up. Saturday was the only night my parents were free to go out and have some fun for themselves.

Dad wore a very 1960's ruffle collar and puffy sleeves and had neatly trimmed sideburns. Mom was dressed in a mini-skirt and shiny white go-go boots. But I knew I had just as much fun as they did.

Nonny, as I called my grandmother, went all out for my weekly visits. Shortly after Mom and Dad dropped me off, dinner would be served. I loved her carrots. Sliced thick and never mushy, they swam in a sea of drawn butter and melted in my mouth like candy. "Orange wheels," I called them, which always made her laugh.

Nonny's other specialty was a steaming platter heaped with succulent chicken and rice. I was too young to know that, approaching her mid-eighties, this was the only meal of the week Nonny actually cooked anymore. With her arthritis, it was hard just to open the can of Campbell's mushroom soup she stirred in the rice to give it that special "oomph." And skinning and de-boning the chicken breasts (they were cheaper that way) was a nearly Herculean effort for the little old lady who spent the rest of the week zapping Lean Cuisine dinners and sipping tea with blueberry muffins for dessert.

Nonny had a special set of dishes she'd purchased, one dish a week, at the local grocery store. They were white and covered with blue windmills and those little wooden shoes and called "Dutch" something or other. Nonny told me that she had bought them just for our special dinners, and that I was the only person she ever used them on. This always made me feel ten feet tall. (It was years later before she finally confessed that the real reason she only used them with me was that she'd skipped a few weeks down at the grocery store and the set was incomplete!

Dinner was usually over by the time *The Lawrence Welk Show* came on, and even though it was her favorite show, Nonny said she preferred spending time with her "little man." So we'd retire to the creaky wooden porch swing. Nonny's husband, my grandfather, had died years earlier. The two of them had spent countless hours in this very porch swing, rocking back and forth and admiring the Florida sunset while the neighbor children played, dogs barked, and flowers bloomed. And now it was my turn to sit next to Nonny and while away her lonely Saturday evenings. But it never felt creepy, taking my grandfather's place in that creaky, old porch swing. To me, it just felt right.

While champagne music bubbled through the screen door from the TV, Nonny and I would sit and swing, swing and sit. Sometimes I'd draw and she would sew. Other times, we'd just talk about the neighbors or what each of us had done that day. She'd share stories about growing up in the Great Depression until the closing strains of champagne music were corked for yet another week. Then it was time for dessert, which, in the best of all grandmotherly traditions, was something Mom would never give me at home: a bottle of Coca-Cola, the short kind that fit perfectly into a young boy's hand, and a can of fancy mixed nuts. Nonny showed me how to drop the salty Spanish peanuts inside the bottle and watch the soda fizz and foam, then take a sip, chomping the slimy nuts and tasting the salty sweetness of the fizzy soda.

Nonny called this concoction our "Porch Swing Cocktails," and not only were they delicious, but they made me feel grown up. Imagine a five year-old drinking a cocktail!

When the cokes were gone, we'd chomp on cashews and almonds and listen to dogs bark in the distance. Nonny would light a citronella candle to ward off the mosquitoes, so big and plentiful that she called them Florida's State Bird!

As the night got darker, the tempo of our rocking would gradually slow down, until our feet just dangled in the warm air. We hardly moved at all except for the smooth ocean breeze crawling over us from the beach. living half-a block from the Atlantic Ocean, there wasn't a night of her life that Nonny didn't enjoy falling asleep to the sound of ocean breakers crashing against the sandy beach. She said she wouldn't trade that sound for anything in the world.

Although I am old enough now to enjoy the real alcoholic drink, I sure could go for a Porch Swing Cocktail.

So you see, this is not a "boy, I miss my grandmother story." Although, to be quite honest, it has been quite awhile since I've stopped by Nonny's just for the heck of it. And, although I doubt I could find two real, honest-to-goodness glass "bottles" of Coke, I could swing by the gas station up the street and grab two of those 16-ounce plastic bottles. Of course, with the way I've been packing on the pounds lately, I'd probably go for a DIET Coke. Better grab Nonny one too, all that sugar might give her gas.

And, those nuts aren't all that good for you, I hear, with the fat and the salt. But, maybe just this once...

"A friend is one whom one may pour out all the contents of one's heart..."
-Arabian Proverb

Pop Colombe

Pop
Patty Colombe

I was the only one of eight children in our family to call our father Pop. He was a special man that everyone seemed to love. If I had to describe him, I don't know if I could. He was so many different, wonderful things wrapped up together in this incredible gift named Gilbert.

Pop was a person who watched and listened. His face held the wisdom of his seventy-six years. He served up advice like the richest soup. Only the naive or ignorant wouldn't accept it. And, like a good, hearty soup, his advice was practical without unnecessary frills to overload.

My father was a handsome man whose appearance belied his age. He stood tall and proud. His eyes shone the deepest blue that penetrated your heart to see your thoughts and feel your emotions. A kind man, Pop's judgments were fair and his punishment gentle. This gentleness made the punishment all the worse since disappointing him was the greatest punishment of all.

One thing stood out: his ability to captivate with his stories. I remember listening for hours.

Pop's first language was French. He spoke quickly and sometimes French phrases would mix with English making the stories all the more interesting. Words would flow from his lips effortlessly to weave a delightful tale strewn with threads of fact and fancy. Pop's verbal adventures always left you wanting more.

With animated face and waving hands, he would always tell one more story before bed.

My favorites were his "scary stories." Some he swore to be factual, while other tales would leave you wondering. It's probably how I developed my macabre side.

The following story was always my favorite, even though I had heard it hundreds of times. (Pop swore it was true.)

As a young man, Pop worked in lumber camps. The men working in these camps would often have to live in the woods for months at a time. These "men" were often boys of fourteen or fifteen forging their way in the world or those who had to help their families in order to survive. My father was the latter. His father died when he was fourteen so he became the head of the household. Pop wasn't the oldest, but he

35

was always a caretaker. This continued on throughout his life. He raised his father's family, his own large brood, as well as numerous nieces, nephews, and grandchildren. He loved children, and although he could see their faults, he also marveled in their beauty and innocence. Pop would never allow a child to suffer.

While on one of these logging excursions, he experienced a strange occurrence of which he wove a tale.

At this particular camp, two great friends went off to work together. The camp was located near a town which was several hours away by road but less than an hour by river-crossing. Some of the men would often make the trek to town across the water. A handful of men would go and stumble into their bunks in the early morning hours, or some barely in time for breakfast.

Of these men was one of our two friends. One friend remained serious and hard working. The other, although he worked hard, enjoyed a good time. He was also prone to take chances. Once while crossing the river, the free spirit was so drunk, he fell in. Soaking wet, the wild man couldn't even get into his top bunk, so he rolled into the bottom bunk with his friend. The slumbering friend awoke cursing and complaining that he would only be able to do half his usual work when the sun rose. The complaints fell on deaf, sleeping ears.

One evening, after a hard day's work at the camp, the fun loving friend made ready for his regular journey. The weather had been unpredictable over the previous week, and the other hearty souls decided not to go.

Heavy rain had caused the river to rise dangerously. This didn't deter our friend. The chance to meet young women on the other side seemed worth the risk.

Some time through the night, the serious young man could feel something wet and cold get into his bed.

"You fell in the river again, didn't you?" was all he said, and pulled as far as he could to the side of the bed and went back to sleep.

In the morning, the sensible friend rose and made ready for work. Oddly, his friend had already left.

The wanderer wasn't at breakfast. It was unusual he would start before anyone else. Nor was he anywhere else. After a few minutes, the eating ritual was interrupted.

Several men rushed in shouting that there was something down by the river. Everyone gathered around. There, washed up on the shore, was the body of the adventurous friend.

Pop swore it was a true story. The serious young man was said to never venture into the lumber camps afterward.

Curiously, Pop started working with a road construction company the spring following the incident. Pop never worked in the lumber camps again.

I'd often ask who was the young man who wouldn't venture into town. He'd just smile with a twinkle in his blue eyes. Then, he'd start another story.

In memory of Gilbert 'Pop' Colombe. A void remains since you left this world that can never be filled.

"Fairy Tale, n.: A horror story to prepare children for the newspapers."

"D" Day
Cindy F. Ovard

A stream of tears coursed down my twelve-year-old face as my dad held me tightly in his arms for the last time in our family home. We had gathered together as a family for family prayer as we had done each and every weekday morning, but this time it was different. Mom and Dad were going through a "D". The big D word, a divorce. See! I got it out finally. Did I say that word out loud to anyone? I was afraid to say that word to any of my friends. What would they say and think? Would they still like me? Could I still go to church on Sunday and look everyone in the face? Our small town hadn't had many divorces. In fact, I didn't have a single friend with divorced parents.

We had been considered stalwart members of our community and our church. We had seven children and two hard working, reliable parents. We were known as a great family. I was number three in the line up of kids. Family prayer and Family Home Evening's were part of our every day and weekly activities. We didn't drink coffee or tea, herb tea was OK, but who wanted tea that tasted and smelled like you'd just mowed your grass? We didn't smoke. We didn't even drink Coke or Pepsi, but Root beer was a staple of our family parties. Hires homemade Root beer straight from the five-gallon drum seeping with steaming, haunting looking dry ice. We didn't have pierced ears or wear shorts shorter than our kneecaps. We were stalwart in our Mormon faith.

So how could this be happening to our family? Why was this happening to our family?" My mom kept telling me this was the way it needed to be. To trust her that this was the answer The answer to what?

I walked out of the house along side my dad as he placed his arm around my shoulders. He was crying and kept asking my mom to please not do this. He didn't want to leave his children, his family, nor his childhood home. This was his town. He had grown up here. His best friends lived here. This town was his life. My father's family had helped settle this pioneer town. My mother, on the other hand, was the "outsider". Her family had moved here during her last year of High school in 1951. She hadn't known anyone. When they met at a pep rally my father had introduced her to all of his friends; to his town, to his way of life and now she was asking him to leave it all and not come back.

Dad grabbed hold of the door handle of his old Chevy truck and turned around to look at us. His eyes went to my mother who stood on the front porch carrying my little baby brother on her hip. Dad's eyes pleaded with her begging her to let him stay, but she just turned her head and went back into the house. I had never seen my dad cry before; I started bawling. My brothers and sisters sat on the front porch steps sobbing in-between heavy breaths. Dad walked up to each of us and hugged each in turn. We talked very quietly amongst ourselves. He told us to be good to our mom and do what she said. He climbed into the truck and started the engine. As he drove off he waved out the window. I ran after him for a full block crying and yelling out his name.

I watched as the truck rounded the corner and I couldn't see it any longer. It had been loaded with Dad's personal stuff. An old table that I had seen in the dark old attic the week was to be used for a kitchen table. I saw old rickety chairs and a few odds and ends piled high in the back. These were to help him set up a place to call home. He got the old couch from the TV room and a chair that belonged to his dad with an ottoman. It didn't matter that we had three other couches in better condition; he still got the crappy old stuff. Maybe he took it because he felt he wouldn't be gone long and Mom would come to her senses sooner or later, but sooner or later never happened. Dad still kept the shoddy old stuff and tried to make the best of it!

Our daily scripture study ended, as well as our daily family prayer. My oldest brother went to live with Dad in "The Pad" as my mom referred to it. Two single guys living life to the hilt. My brother had just graduated from High School and needed to live on his own for awhile. He tried to reassure me of family life, but I didn't want reassurance I wanted my family back. I wanted my dad back home with us to bring safety and security back in my life.

The local church members took the news badly. My mother soon became the woman who wore the scarlet letter, except her letter was a "D". Some folks were in total shock and I read pity on their faces.

I wasn't going to be the victim of their pity. I wasn't going to let them get to me. I was a survivor. I picked up books to read. All kinds of books. I lived at the library and read every Nancy Drew and Hardy Boy's mystery I could find. Reading opened up a whole new realm of adventure. My love of reading is what made me realize I wanted to be a writer someday.

Their divorce was finalized six months later and we were definitely on our own. Dad tried to move to a small house just down the street from us, but Mom wouldn't go for that. She wanted him far away and not to bother her at all. He moved back to the big city about an hour from us and settled into his pad again.

Would I grow up to get divorced just like my parents? What kind of statistic was I now? We had turned into a sad growing number of single parent families. But, I wasn't alone in this; it seemed after my mom got her divorce; the whole town went berserk. More and more families started splitting up. My mom set a trend for our small town, not a happy trend either.

I spent many nights crying myself to sleep and wondering why I had to be in a family that got divorced. One night after my prayers and crying, I looked out my bedroom window and saw a shooting star. I wished on it. My wish was just for some kind of peace and some kind of assurance that I was going to be OK, that my family would be OK. I was only twelve years old and I felt The Lord answer my prayer in my heart. "Be strong and don't give up," He said. I felt peace and calmness come over me.

I learned from that time on that He listens even to the smallest of his children. He listened to me and answered my prayer.

D-day proved to be a very sad time in my life, but I have learned to make those sad times strengths in my life. I will not be a victim of my past. I am happy and look back on my childhood with great fondness and great memories.

"To the family—that dear octops from whose tentacles we never quite escape, nor, in our inmost hearts, ever quite wish to."
-Dodie Smith

40

Lela Bush and Joseph DeLaurentis

February 1944
Lela Eitel

My friend asked me if I'd like to accompany her to a dance with her sister and friend on Saturday night. Wow! Would I? My friend Mary was 17 and I was only 15, but I had been yearning to find out about the ways of the world. As far as my parents knew, I was spending the night with Mary and would be home in the morning.

My first problem was deciding what to wear. What does one wear to a dance hall, I wondered. "Pretty casual," said Mary.

I decided on my red pleated skirt and a white mohair sweater that was already in my wardrobe, but what kind of shoes? This was important because if I danced I couldn't wear totter heels. I knew I couldn't wear my saddle shoes and therefore I'd have to do some shopping.

My income was limited. The shoes would have to be cheap. They couldn't be high heels or I'd never make it to the dance floor. What I chose was a pair of red shoes made of a grosgrain type of fabric.

Saturday night finally arrived and we boarded a bus with a sign reading, Shadowland." It was crowded and noisy. Fortunately, we found seats. Latecomers had to hang from straps, swaying with the ride.

Joe, a sergeant with insignias of the 702nd tank battalion, happened to be one of the swayers nearby. When he saw me, it was love at first sight, or so he told me later. He never took his eyes of me the rest of the evening.

That was certainly exciting for me, but, at the same time, I knew enough to hold him at arm's length while deciding if he was trustworthy.

After several more dates I felt like we'd known each other for years. I knew I could trust him completely. Yet, it was wartime and all too soon his unit was shipped out. Our courtship, if it continued, had to be by mail.

During the following year my life centered on the mail, news of war-torn Europe where Joe was-somewhere. He couldn't tell me or even hint at where he was. All letters were censored. By studying the news and his letters, I arrived at the conclusion that he was in Patton's 3rd Army and in France.

I was right. Then, his unit moved up into Luxembourg. He wrote as often as possible. He remembered our first meeting, our first dance, our first kiss. He remembered those red shoes, of all things. He said, "Honey, when I saw those shoes, I wondered about you." That made me laugh.

Joe wanted to come home so badly. He was so homesick. He had taken cold and his feet were given him problems from being so cold and frozen in the tank for hours on end. On February 14th, he received our Valentine's, one from me, my sister, and my mom. He wrote how much they meant to him. He didn't tell me that he'd gone to the medics about his feet. I found out about that later.

The mail was so slow. I'd wait and nearly die a thousand deaths before a letter arrived. In the meantime, we'd hear the news reports and I'd consider if the incident was near my Joe and if he might be involved.

My usual habit was to arrive home from my after-school job, around eight p.m. I'd walk over to the large oak piano and check the mail. I'd be so happy to see the striped envelope or the small V-mail stationary. This meant news from Joe.

Then one night in March, a few weeks after Valentine's Day, I found a note from my mother. No mail from Joe. I took it into my room and read it. The house was still and dark. My mother had received a call from someone, who remains a mystery yet today, that told her that Joe had been killed on February 18th, as he drove his tank into Germany.

There's no way to explain how I took the news. I wanted to deny it but I knew it had to be true. Joe's mother had been writing to me since Christmas and had received a telegram at about the same time. She was devastated. Joe was her only son and she'd prayed so hard for his safe return.

We corresponded for about another fifteen years, but somehow we lost track of one another. She's always promised she'd send me a picture of his grave but she didn't Later I learned that she had spent a lot of time in the hospital. Neither of us ever got over Joe's death.

My life went on. I married and had a family, but the memory of Joe has remained all these years. I found his grave and some of his family in 1995 when I accompanied one daughter to Philadelphia, his old hometown.

Joseph Francis DeLaurentis is one hero of WWII. For all the heroes we need to be grateful for their defending us and leaving us the freedom and ability to live in peace. Joe gave all he could for what he believed in. He told me, "Honey, first comes God, then country, then family." That's how he lived and died.

Any man's death diminishes me, because I am involved in mankind; And therefore never send to know for whom the bell tolls; it tolls for thee."

-John Donne

Wilma Claire Hathaway and Bernice Belle Hathaway

"We ought to do good to others as simply as the horse runs, or a bee makes honey, or a vine bears grapes season after season without thinking of the grapes it has borne."
    -Marcus Aurelius

The Bee Tree

V. Arlene Woodhouse Smith Frodey

At age 88 years old, and suffering some memory loss, my mother Wilma Hathaway Woodhouse, suddenly remembered when she was a child, going with her father Lynn A. Hathaway to hunt for bee trees.

Mother remembers, when she was a very young girl, walking for great distances into the woods near the family farm in Big Prairie, Newaygo, Michigan. Grandpa Hathaway made a device to attract a bee that would guide them to a honey tree. It was a wooden stake with a shallow box on top, (about 6 inches square and 1 inch high). He filled the box with some old honey comb, if they had any, and also some anise (liquid) on it. With a compass in hand, Grandpa would watch, and when a bee came to the box, they would see what direction it took as it flew into the woods. Then with compass in hand and little Wilma hurrying along behind, as fast as her little legs would carry her, Grandfather would watch his compass and follow the bees path in a straight line, (hence the term "bee line"). Mother remembers it seemed like a long, long walk, but she was so happy to be included in such an important task the she didn't complain much.

When they found the bee tree, Grandpa, wearing a net over his hat, would saw the tree down. It was always a big hollow tree. They would then walk the long distance back to the farm house.

The next day, Grandpa would carry a cross cut saw, and Grandma loaded down with buckets and large pans, would set out to find the bee tree and gather the honey. Grandma and Grandpa, would be wearing hats with nets, long sleeves and gloves to protect their hands. They would scoop the honey into the pans. Mother said that even with the nets over their hats and clothing to protect them they got stung now and then.

Back at the farm house, the usually barefoot children had to be very careful not to step on the still live bees that came back in the honey. Mother remembers they were everywhere. She also remembers that the honey required straining, and that dark honey was from older hives and the lighter honey was from newer bee hives.

This story told by Wilma Hathaway Woodhouse, now 92 years old, to her daughter, V. Arlene Woodhouse Smith Frodey.

Poppie

Poppie's Photo
Michael D. Arnold

It was always my favorite photo. The photo depicted a man standing in front of a Quonset hut, one arm hanging loosely at his side, the other resting on the hilt of the gun hanging on his hip. The clothes he wore were standard issue fatigues from World War ii, but they were dusty, faded, and worn. By his stance and his casual grin, he seemed comfortable with the life style. A Colt .45 was strapped to his side, with a white mother-of-pearl handle, gleaming slightly in the sunlight. The holster hung from a web belt. It had straps hanging down his thigh to tie it down, but they hung there unused. He wasn't a particularly good-looking man, but ruggedly handsome. With dark hair, a weather-beaten face from months of exposure to the sun, and day old beard from not shaving, he made for one tough looking soldier. The picture itself was slightly faded, with a few water stains, and one corner missing, actually cutting off a portion of the legs of the man in the photo. The missing corner was probably eaten away by insects, or torn away accidently. The photo was only 5" x 7", but it was large enough to see the dunes in back of the hut, and the men relaxing in the cool shade of the trees. It looked like any day would, in the hot tropical African climate.

When my grandmother asked what things in the house were dear to me, the photo and the gun immediately came to mind. I could think of nothing else that I would cherish as much. Grandmother carefully placed the photo in a large envelope. Then, we both walked to the rear of the house, where my Grandfather stored all his guns. She opened the cabinet, took down a small shoe box, and carefully handed it to me. We walked back to the living room and I opened the box. There lay the gun Poppie wore in the photo.

While examining the gun, we noticed that the mother-of-pearl handles were now replaced with plastic white ones. However, the leather holster remained in incredible condition for its age, still soft and supple to the touch. A bold U.S." stamp on the front flap, and the "1908" on the back were still very visible. It was fairly close to being a cavalry holster, like those one might see in western films at the turn of the century.

While reminiscing with my Grandmother, I brought to mind how Poppie told me of his adventures in Africa and Europe. On one occasion Poppie and I were horseback riding to search for some cattle that had slipped through his fence line. He mentioned names of people I had only heard of in movies of that time—Rommell, Montgomery, and Churchill, to name just a few. He told me another story of German tanks in the Black Forest of Germany at the Battle of the Bulge. He then looked down at our horses and laughed as he recalled the time he and friends had to resort to eating horse meat for sustenance when supplies had run low. Later, he even stooped low in his saddle to simulate how the slithering of the huge snakes his unit had encountered in Africa. The snakes would hide in the water waiting for the men as they waded across. It took six men to wrestle a snake off the pour soul who happened to step on one.

Both Poppie and his brother were stationed in Africa during the war, although they were in different areas. As much as my grandfather loved to tell tales, his brother was the exact opposite, never speaking of his time in the War.

Christmas was getting closer, and as always I grasped for ideas of what gifts to get my family and friends. For my Grandmother, I eventually came to the conclusion that giving her a larger version of that picture would be a nice surprise. Of course, now I had to recall where I had left the photo. Like most people, I had boxes and boxes of photographs, but I usually kept the special ones in one particular box. I sifted through it slowly, and as expected, it wasn't there. Once the photo was found, I then delivered it to a company for restoration. It took several weeks, but once the work was completed, it was impossible to tell the photo had ever been damaged.

While the photo was being restored, I decided to search for some replacement grips for the pistol. The mother-of-pearl handles would have been impossible to replace at a reasonable price. So I settled on some checkered walnut grips made by a gentleman in Arizona. His specialty was creating replacement parts for classic weapons. As soon as I received them, I placed them on the gun, and mounted it in a display case I had purchased. This case was only slightly more difficult to find than the grips.

I attempted to find a frame that matched the many picture frames she already had, and the antique photographs around her home. After carefully searching various shops in the area, I finally purchased a beautiful antique frame that went well with that style photograph. I then placed the photo in the frame, and carefully wrapped it in Christmas paper.

Everyone knew what I would give Grandmother for Christmas, and they were all excited to see her reaction. When she finally opened her gift, her eyes grew very large, and tears began to well up in them.

She carefully placed the photo down on the coffee table. Clasping me tightly in her arms, she attempted to squeeze the life out of me.

Several days later, my Grandmother sat me down, and with a smile told me she had a confession to make. I sat down, and quietly waited for this confession that had her so obviously amused. She softly took my hands in hers, and explained that the photo was not my Grandfather. Surprised at this revelation, I quickly smiled to make sure she knew I wasn't upset. She remarked that as children we had all assumed the photo was of our Grandfather, but was in fact, a photo of his brother, my Uncle Johnny. They were difficult to tell apart at that age, especially in a black and white photo. We all got such a thrill imaging the photo was of our Grandfather, that she did not have the heart to tell s otherwise. If anything, I actually thought the situation incredibly funny. I wasn't surprised that we would have assumed such a thing, given the fact that Poppie had filled our minds with so many tales.

Each time I look at my copy of the photo and the gun mounted in a glass case, I still think of my Grandfather. The confession didn't change the love that I feel for my Grandmother or Grandfather. If anything, it just strengthened our bond. When anyone asks me about the photo, I say, that until recently, it was a photo of my Grandfather. They usually look at me funny for a few seconds and then ask for an explanation. That always makes for a far more interesting story.

"The virtue of the camera is not the power it has to transform the photographer into an artist, but the impulse it gives him to keep on looking."
-Brooks Atkinson

Grandma Mary Iovino

Good Memories and Better Memories
Esther DiLuca

It was a time, the late-1940s, when children were "seen and not heard." Adults ruled the roost and children were obedient. Adults commanded great respect—or is the more appropriate word "demanded!" Our late, paternal Grandma Mary left us with many fond memories, but the credit for my first encounter with deception also goes to her. Many times when we sisters get together, especially on holidays, and start to reminisce on our childhood, the talk usually ends up with "and remember when...."

Grandma Mary's house was separated from ours by a fence and was actually an extension of my parents' property, so as children we often scooted back-and-forth to visit. We would often swing with Grandma in her hammock and idle away the long summer days mostly listening to her reminisce of her childhood days in the old country. If she spoke too fast, as she often did, we would have a difficult time understanding her broken English. It would irritate her if we asked her to repeat something—never could figure out if she thought she didn't have our full attention or she was getting a message that she wasn't speaking perfect English.

On the summer days, when it was not too hot, we would go blueberry picking, which we loved to do so she could bake those luscious berry pies that we would enjoy on our next visit. Or, if it was, indeed, too hot for berry picking, we would just go for long walks, or just help her pick some of her vegetables—grandma always had a vegetable garden. She was a very tall, striking-looking woman with dyed platinum hair—which I think now was a little ahead of her time. I suppose, too, a sense of humor--which was a little ahead of our time— and which escaped our then young ages of 6 or 7 years. One of the words that was totally unacceptable to her was "no." If she asked you to do a chore—she didn't particularly like washing her floors or her windows, run an errand to the corner store, or whatever the moment required, there was no response acceptable to her but, "of course."

Upon visiting her one particular hot summer's day, she had apparently decided that her vegetable garden needed to be weeded. Her garden always consisted of tomatoes and string beans—what I call the itchy plants. Have you ever experienced having these leaves touch your bare skin—your arms or legs--and on a hot summer's day? You'll itch until you take to soap and water. Since it was too hot for her to do this chore (maybe she didn't want to deal with the itching), she asked my younger sister and me if we would weed for her. Not being particularly interested in that chore either, we stated so—rather directly and clearly, I suspect. Our decision, however, was not one she was about to accept, so she resorted to another ploy.

She went indoors and returned with a large box of chocolates and proceeded to tell us that if we'd weed her garden we could have our choice of these large, delectable chocolates—but no peeking! Hey, these were "Candy Cupboard" chocolates —they didn't get any better in those days! She hit our weak spot, so we consented to her wishes in spite of the oppressive heat. Anticipating just how delicious the chocolates were going to taste, we did a pretty fair job weeding-- around those itchy plants! When finished, we announced to Grandma that we were ready for our surprise piece--or was it pieces--of candy. A surprise, indeed!

I don't know what devastated us more, the disappointment of not getting what we had expected—large chocolates—or the fact that this adult, whom we had so thoroughly admired and believed, tricked us! For, indeed, what was supposed to have been our surprise of a large, "Candy Cupboard" chocolate was a "Hershey's Chocolate Chip"!

"Grandma Mary!" "Chocolate Chips are not served—they go into chocolate chip cookies. Who ate the chocolates that we thought we were going to get?" This was not a fair exchange—definitely not a fair deal. "We've been tricked, and we hope you realize you've made us feel bad! We'll not come back to see you any time soon!"

But soon, almost too soon, the aroma of those pies came wafting through the warm summer evening helping us to forget very quickly the work, and the sweat, and the itching, and the large chocolates we didn't get! Oh, yes indeed, she knew exactly how to get us back into her good graces! But, would the pie taste as sweet?

Today, my sisters and I laugh about this whenever it's mentioned, and I suppose mostly we laugh because we still think it was an incredible thing to have done to us. I would think that if that was her sense of humor, after she enjoyed her joke, she should have awarded us with what we had expected, but that wasn't done.

I know, back then, it was instant mistrust and a long time before thoroughly trusted her word again. However, the time it took us to return for Grandma Mary's pies was a lot shorter, which probably helped considerably in giving her the love and respect that she really deserved—or commanded—or demanded.

Do adults often forget how to think at a child's level? Do adults dismiss little things as unimportant? Do children recognize deception? It takes a lot of years before children mature to adulthood and cultivate the perspective to assign "things" to proper and significant order. We all have **good** memories; we should leave **better** memories for the future.

"As with most fine things, chocolate has its season. There is a simple memory aid that you can use to determine whether it is the correct time to order chocolate dishes: any month whose name contains the letter A, , or U is the proper time for chocolate.
-Sandra Boynton

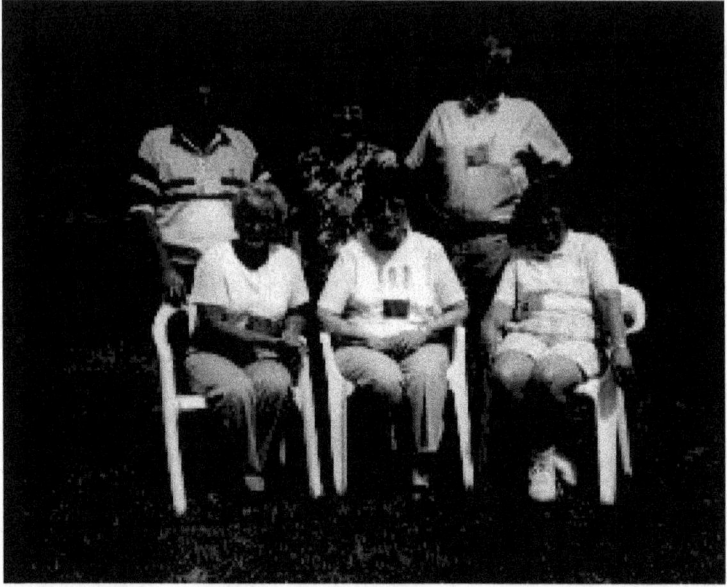

John Kelly's brother and sister: (standing) Francis, Rose,
John (seated) Mary, Ginny, Teresa

Kelly Family Farm Celebrates 100 Years

MaryBeth Thayer

On Sunday June 27, 1999 approximately 150 descendants of William and Regina Kelly gathered to celebrate the Kelly family farm's 100th birthday. The 160 acre Kelly farm located 5 miles southwest of Murdock is currently owned by John Kelly, grandson of William and Regina. The plans for the celebration sprung out of a conversation that John had had with his cousin Father Joel (Joseph) Kelly about five years ago.

"We were talking about how the farm would be 100 years old in about three or four years and I had stated that maybe we should have everybody out here for a party and you can say a mass," John recalled.

Taking John at his suggestion plans for a celebration were begun. Mike Kelly, John and Pam's son, began collecting information for the family tree. By the fall of 1998 a web site was created to display not only the family tree but also to give updated reports on the plans and details of the upcoming celebration. This day's celebration began with coffee and rolls at 10:00 a.m. which was followed by catered meal at noon. The events of the reunion and celebration were capped with a centenary mass led by cousin Father Joel in mid afternoon. Cars arrived in a steady trickle during the morning hours; each one carrying people who had a link to the legacy of William and Regina. Relatives renewed their bonds to each other with hugs and kisses. Pictures were shared and family stories were relived with tears and laughter. The enduring legacy of William and Regina was once again revisited.

Retelling the Beginning

With video cameras rolling 86 year old Mary Kelly Kennedy, the second youngest child of William and Regina related the story of how her parents came to Murdock.

"My mother, Regina Schwingler, lived in Medalia and worked as a seamstress. Her work as a seamstress had her traveling to the homes of her clients and living with them while she sewed. Later she worked at a store as a clerk. My father, William Kelly, lived near St. James working on a dairy farm. They met and were married on May 25, 1899. It was the money that mother had saved that helped to make a down payment on the farm," stated Mary.

Coming to the Murdock area by horse and buggy the pair purchase a 160 acre farm southwest of town. Located on the property's most southwestern corner was a three room house. The house was moved to it's present site with a team of horses and big logs.

"The process took several days and mother said that she cooked the meals as the house was moving," Mary recounted.

Of course additions to the house were made as the family grew to number eight children: Stanley, Isabelle, Emily, Howard, Ruth Helen Mary and Ben.

"Tell again the difference between grandpa and grandma," asked Virginia White and Rose Kelly, granddaughters of William and Regina and daughters of their son, Howard.

"Well mother was German and very strict. She worked hard and everything had to be just so. Father on the other hand was Irish and just as hard working but he had a soft side. I remember one time when Isabelle and Emily had been out late on dates. The following morning mother gave them a hard time for coming in late but when dad walked into the kitchen the first thing he asked was, "So did you have fun last night?"

That was the difference between mother and dad. My father loved the farm and he loved us kids. More than once he came to bat for us kids. Never once did I hear my parents argue. If they did, we kids didn't know about it or maybe they argued somewhere else, I don't know. But if mother didn't get her way she could pout for days. I remember when the milk machine was purchased before the radio. Mother went into the bedroom and shut the door. She stayed there for quite a while too. We then got a radio, one of those that had to have its antenna put on the roof of the house," Mary explained with a smile.

When reading a book of family recollections and memories written by Mary Kennedy one thing becomes crystal clear, the work was hard but all worked together. The younger children and the elder sisters helped with the housework and gardening. Father and the elder sons farmed the land and milked the cows. Fun times were had in the midst of the work.

"We always had company of some sort. When I look back I don't know how my mother ever did it. There was the time that we housed the school teacher for a year. And another time we had 23 people stay over night and with none of the modern conveniences. Where did she put us all?" she recalled with a shake of her head.

The Kelly farm was one of the first in the area to have registered Holsteins in its dairy. William served on the boards that helped to

56

establish the Murdock Farmers' Elevator in 1909 and the Farmers' Creamery.

"Mother valued education. She wanted to be a nurse and couldn't because there wasn't enough money. So she made sure each of a kids had a chance to go to college and get an education. And we did. I remember when I was in teaching school and overwhelmed by all the work. I called mother and asked her if I could come home. She said, "Sure you can come home but just remember this is your only chance to go to school." I stayed and finished," Mary commented.

"And that has hung with us, " was the consensus of those sitting in the living room of the 100 year old house.

A change of hands

In 1929 William Kelly passed away. Regina took the children yet at home and moved to Murdock. Howard Kelly married Catherine Esther McGovern and moved to family farm to take over operations. In addition he purchased another farm located just south of the Kelly family farm. To this union nine children were born: Theresa Louise (passed away at age 14 due to scarlet fever), Virginia Ann, Catherine, John, Rose Mary, Mary Celeste, Francis, Joseph (passed away soon after birth) and Teresa Marie (named after her older sister).

"I remember grandma writing a letter quite soon after grandpa's death. It started with the phrase, "Just in case I do not have time to make out a will," recalled Virginia. "The letter went on to state and discuss matters of the farm and so forth.

"She wrote two of those letters," added Mary Kennedy. "The second one was written 30 years later as she was getting older. You know she didn't sell the farm to Howard until a year before she died which was in 1958. I think that all she really wanted was to make sure the farm stayed in the family."

A murmur of agreement and the nods of those participating in the conversation confirmed the accuracy of the idea.

"I remember on Sundays after church I would go along with dad (Howard) to Grandma's and together they would sit and discuss the farm business," stated John.

"Yes, I remember that too," added Virginia. "There would only be one of us allowed to go with dad at a time and during the visit we had to sit very still."

"You know she was concerned about your dad paying for the farm," spoke Mary.

Yes and I remember hearing dad say to her don't worry about it; we'll take care of it," finished John.

"Mother was a business woman right to the end," commented Mary and then she went on to say, "This day is so special I just have a feeling that my parents know this is going on."

The farm continues

And as the farm changed hands the seasons passed. The cows were milked and the crops were planted and harvested and the children of Howard and Esther (as she was called) roller skated around the dining room table in between their daily chores.

"Mom would have hired girls to help her with the work. Often times these girls were just a few years older than us and they were fun to play games with.," stated Virginia. "I remember one time when I asked my mom if the hired girl could come and play ball with us. Boy, did I ever get a look from Mom. Those girls were there to work."

A chuckle rippled throughout the room.

"What about the time that you showed Catherine how to drive, John?" asked Rose.

John shook his head, "Catherine wanted to learn how to drive and I already had my license. Mom was washing clothes and dad was cultivating corn. We got into the car and said we were going to go around half a section. We had to turn around half way around the section because if we went completely around, dad, who was cultivating on the southwest corner of the farm, would see us."

"I remember watching you two leave the yard," added Virginia. "And then you didn't come back and when you didn't come back I began to wonder what happened. Then the neighbor's car drove up into the yard and you two got out."

"Yes, as we were turning around to come home the back wheels of the car got caught in the gravel and the car tipped over into the ditch. Dad was upset," finished John.

"Yes," Teresa nodded her head in agreement. "But do you remember what mom said to him? Now don't yell at the kids. They might be in shock. Mom would use that phrase every once in a while when one of us kids was hurt to calm him down or maybe to protect us, I don't know which."

"You know for all the years I lived on the farm I never saw a calf born," remembered Virginia. "Dad would always send us girls up to the house if anything like that was going to happen. I never saw a birth until after I was married."

"My mother always protected us kids from that too," added Mary with a chuckle.. "A cat was having her kittens on the front steps of the house and mother had the boys put in a box and take it down to the barn."

Kelly farm in the present

After John, Howard's son, returned from his term of military service, he and his wife Pam (Iverson) moved to his father's farm located just south of the original Kelly farm. John took over the dairy operations and helped with the crop farming. During the winter of 1965 - 1966 the snowstorms were so bad that many times Howard was required to do the milking. The next spring it was decided that John and his wife Pam should move to the original Kelly farm. And so it was that one more generation of Kellys was to know the family stead as home. This new generation of Kellys; Laura, Regina, Michael and Maria, would grow up to become actively involved in 4-H and get the college education so stressed by their great grandmother Regina. And during the entire process their father John remarked, "I was under the cows and farming and loving every minute of it."

As John gradually took over reins of the farm operation from his father Howard the raising of chickens and pigs was eliminated and the concentration remained on solely on dairy and crop production.

"There was hardly never a time when there weren't dairy cattle on the place," John stated. "Maybe once for a couple of years when I was in the service. We started out the herd with 27 cows and then increased it to 50 cows."

In 1992 John declared himself retired from the dairy herd but not from the land. Each year he continues to put in a crop and harvest.

"Farm technology has gotten so much better. It is not near the physically demanding work that it used to be."

And just what plans, if any, are there for the Kelly farm in an age where the move is towards larger farms and corporate farming?

With strong assurance John states, "I'm not selling out. It's going to stay in the family."

First published in *Kerkhoven Banner* (MN).

"We do not inherit this land from our ancestors; we borrow it from our children."
-Haida Indian saying

Anthony Crawford

The Lynching of Anthony Crawford
Doria Dee Johnson

I am the great-great granddaughter of Anthony and Tebby Crawford, the great granddaughter of George and Annabelle Crawford, the granddaughter of Joseph and Fannie Crawford Brooks, the daughter of Dr. Charles and Helen Brooks Johnson. This story is about my great-great grandfather's lynching in 1916. He was murdered in Abbeville, SC by a crowd estimated between 200 and 400 blood thirsty people. His ordeal lasted all day. His body was beaten and drug through town to show other Negroes what would happen to them if they got "insolvent". Finally, he was taken to the county fair grounds and strung up to a tree and riddled with bullets. Although, we have heard his body was thrown in someone's lawn, we have yet to locate his grave. The family was ordered to vacate their land and get out of town. They did just that. We are still searching for family members, although some returned. What was his crime you might ask? Cursing a white man for offering him a low price for the cottonseed he was trying to sell and being too rich for a Negro.

Anthony P. Crawford was born in January 1865 and owned by Ben and Rebecca Crawford in Abbeville, South Carolina. He proved to be quite a scholar and walked 7 miles and back to school each day. When Anthony finished school, he was a laborer for Ben Crawford. When his father Thomas died, Anthony was the only one of nine siblings to sign his own name: the others signed with X's. His father, Thomas Crawford starting acquiring plots of land evidenced by the 1880 census. By 1893, Thomas died and left some land to Anthony. At the time of his death, Anthony had 427 acres of the "prettiest cotton land in the county".

Andy, as he was known, had 13 children-- all of whom lived on his land with their spouses and children. He built a school on his land for the children of blacks in Abbeville. He held an office with the Masons of South Carolina. He was secretary and chief financial prop of Chapel AME Church for nineteen years. In October of 1894, he was Assistant Marshall of a grand parade in which some 1500 to 2000 persons assembled by trades. The Honorable George W. Murray, the only black US Congressman, was the guest speaker. In August of 1888, the local newspaper reported that he sold three wagons of splendid melons and found there was as much money in them as cotton. In

December of 1904, the *Abbeville Medium* reported:

> *Anthony P. Crawford, colored, sold a load of splendid corn of his own raising in the city last week. His fat mules, good wagon and prosperous appearances led us to inquire particularly about his crop. He farms and owns the old Belcher place. He holds in his own right 500 acres of land in three tracts, paid for by his own labor. This year his corn crop was 1000 bushels, of which he sold 250. He made 200 gallons of syrup and 48 bales of cotton. November 26th he sold $662.08 worth of cotton and has made other sales. He has six horses, 12 head of cattle, 18 hogs, two good wagons, a McCormick rake, and a new top buggy. He also has a good bank account and a family of 13 children.*

By 1916, Andy Crawford was the wealthiest Negro farmer in those parts. His holdings were at least 10% of all land owned by Negroes in the county. There is evidence that he had servants in the household. He would loan whites money between harvest and had changed his crop from cotton before the white farmers did-- because of the boll weevil. His estimated worth was $20,000 dollars, which calculates to $300,000 in 1998. He was a law-abiding citizen and proud.

On the morning of October 21, 1916, Andy rode his horse and buggy into town to W.D. Barksdale's store. Cottonseed was selling at 90 cents a bushel but Barksdale offered Andy only 85 cents. Andy told Mr. Barksdale that he was already given a better offer and before he could gather his seed and leave, Barksdale called him a liar. Andy cursed him and told him he was trying to cheat him and would take his seed elsewhere. The two men argued in the street in front of town square. A store clerk heard the commotion and came out with an ax handle. Andy backed off toward the square and was arrested for cursing Mr. Barksdale. By the time the Sheriff and he reached the jail, word had gotten out that a Negro had cursed a white man and crowds started gathering in the square. Once the crowd dispersed, he paid his bail and the sheriff let him out of a side door to avoid any more commotion. He was headed for a gin, a short distance away when he was spotted by a crowd. When he heard the mob behind him, he hid in a boiler room of a gin and picked up a four-pound hammer. McKinnley Cann, reportedly somewhat of a rouge and the ring leader, led the crowd towards Andy. When they found him, he picked up the hammer and crushed the skull of Cann and would've killed him had someone not grabbed his arm. The crowd proceeded to kick in his teeth. Sheriff Burts had come and begged the crowd not to kill him. He agreed to keep Andy in jail until they were assured that Cann would survive his injuries. While in jail, Andy asked for a doctor and told a friend to get his coat from the gin and give his bankbook to his family. He remarked " I thought I was a good citizen."

In the meantime, the crowd took over the jail, dragged him out onto the square where he regained consciousness, got on his feet and fought while being dragged for 50 feet up the road before being hit with a rock in the back of his head. 200 white men kicked him, beat him, tied him to the back of a buggy, rode him through the black neighborhoods and strung him to a tree and unloaded 200 rounds into what was left of his body.

The governor of South Carolina, Richard I. Manning, was said to be furious and summoned Sheriff Burts. This was a *rich* black man that was lynched this time and he needed some answers. The press was getting hold of the story of this brutal crime and major newspapers were carrying editorials of the horrendous murder in Abbeville. Governor Manning ordered an investigation and promised that the lynchers would be put on trial. He sent in Roy Nash, secretary of the NAACP, for the investigation. Nash had to act as if he was interested in buying land in Abbeville so he could get close to those involved. He discovered that those responsible had closed all black businesses, except one. Nash, also, found out about the order given by the lynchers that the Crawford family leave town immediately or be killed. The night of the lynching, the Crawford boys waited in trees with guns for the lynchers to come to their homestead as promised. They never came. However the Crawfords did leave Abbeville. So did enough of Abbevilles' black population to make almost the whole black population of my hometown, Evanston, IL. Almost everyone black in my hometown has ties to Abbeville. There was a mass exodus right after the lynching and serious economic ramifications followed. Even Ralph Ellison, father of the author Ralph Ellison who wrote: *Invisible Man,* left. The editorials of the day reflect the feeling that the South would pay dearly for making it uncomfortable for blacks to remain. Some Crawfords returned later. Andy's estate listed his heirs as follows and the places where they resided in 1918:

Walter...35 New York City, NY
Minnie...25 died in Abbeville, 1918
Charles..33 Abbeville
George...22 Evanston, IL
Wes...31 Abbeville, SC
Jessie...21 Philadelphia, PA
McGowan...30 Abbeville
Bessie...21 Philadelphia. PA

Julius...29 Abbeville
Anthony,jr...19 Eustis, FL
Florence...27 Abbeville
Albert...16 Philadelphia, PA
Thomas...13 Abbeville

This information was obtained from historians, books, research of census records, interviews. I was always told of the lynching from my maternal grandfather. My great aunt Annabelle has the biggest picture of Anthony Crawford in her home and has been a wealth of knowledge. I've always asked why we never go back to Abbeville to learn more about this great man and my family. They would always say it was too painful. My great uncle Anthony, the last living child of Anthony Crawford, died just a few years ago. He once said "I never want to see Abbeville again as long as I live and would not give Abbeville County a nickel"

While speaking with historians, I am told I am the first Crawford to speak of the lynching and the impact it had on our family. The more I learn, the more I understand the severity of taking away a families' livelihood.

Anthony Crawford was a strong, proud man, who through hard work was becoming quite wealthy. He believed in family, solid education and religion and he built schools and churches. The thought of being so brutally murdered for living an exemplary life in America is unconscionable. It took several generations, but our family is starting to meet each other again. I don't know whether all of his children kept in contact with each other, but I do know my mother was sent to Philadelphia in her childhood summers to visit her great uncle Albert. My cousins in Washington, DC say they went to Abbeville, SC in the summers to visit . My great aunt Eleanor recently told me that my great great uncle Walter, a very successful minister in NYC, visited my grandmothers' home in Evanston, IL before I was born.

In researching the lynching in 1990, I noticed from an article written by Roy Nash, NAACP, that Anthony had been the secretary of Chapel AME Church in Abbeville. I called directory assistance just to see if the church was still there. After calling on a Sunday, to my surprise a young man answered the phone. I told him I was doing some research on my great great grandfather, Anthony Crawford, who belonged to a church by the same name and was lynched in 1916. The phone quickly went silent and then he told me his name was Philip Crawford, the great great grandson of Anthony Crawford. Philip told me of an upcoming reunion of the Crawford family just a few months away in Abbeville. I called my cousin Sandra Crawford-Bailey and we decided to pack up the car and go. Once we arrived, I met cousins from the District of Columbia, New York, Atlanta and all over the United States. We all are descendents of Anthony and Tebby Crawford. We meet almost every year and exchange stories on our famous ancestor's life and death. We met in Virginia Beach, Virginia last year and found out that his story is in countless books, museums and universities. The Crawford clan knows that Anthony's murder was investigated by the state of South Carolina. Anthony Crawford's killers were never brought to trial, although they were brought before the grand jury who decided there was not enough evidence to indict. Crawford's lands were lost because the lynching took away Anthony's children's way of life. Through 2nd mortgages, back taxes, the stock market crash of 1929, and the migration, the Crawfords left couldn't keep up with the payments.

Andy Crawford's legacy is something every African American should be proud of. He once took out an ad in the paper which said :

...and it will be the highest endeavor of our lives, to strive to make as good citizens in the future as we have in the past and to those who opposed and differed with us, I have nothing but a friendly feeling. For individuals as well as nations sometimes differ. But it is mete and right to settle their differences, legally and amicably. A Citizen, Anthony P. Crawford.

My great great grandfather stated early in life, "The day a white man hits me is the day I die". And he did. But he left an example of hard work and determination . He still lives in all of us. Many of us still attend AME Churches and have been told that we have "that arrogant Crawford way". Most of us have obtained our education as set forth by his example. The Crawfords know that those murderers were NOT successful in breaking up the Crawfords. We still stand today proud, close, and live our lives as he would've wanted us to. We will not stop looking for each other until the last Crawford is accounted for and we can stand on his land and look toward heaven and pray that he knows we are together again.

You may read more on Anthony Crawford in the following books:

100 Years of Lynchings by Ralph Ginzberg

From Slavery to Freedom by John Hope Franklin

Old Abbeville ; a history of the town by Dr. Lowry Ware

Bound for the Promised Land: African American Religion & The Great Migration by Milton Sernett

One More Day's Journey by Allen Ballard

Trouble in Mind: Black Southerners in the Age of Jim Crow by Leon F. Litwack

"Ignorance is the parent of fear."
-Hermann Melville

David Conrad Hamilton

Father Dearest

Skylar Burris

Any detached observer might think my father a very laconic man. Indeed, he is rather a recluse, and has never to my knowledge, willingly sought society. He enters sweepstakes, but regrets that if he wins, they will bring T.V. cameras to his very doorstep and expect him to act like a fool for the amusement of thousands of commercial viewers. My brother once asked why he didn't buy a car phone, and he responded, "Why would I? I can't stand people calling me at home, much less when I'm in my car!"

Yet something in the qualities of a recluse makes an excellent father. Perhaps it is that of a man with no friends must at length be driven to share his hopes and his views with his family. Long discussions have highlighted my journey from childhood to maturity. My father, my brother, and I once talked for four hours about the meaning of art and whether or not hell was eternal. My father has never lectured me, but I have learned his morals through these discussions. He has rarely forbidden me to do anything, yet it has always been my instinct to please him. He has rarely refused me anything, and so I asked him for nothing he could not easily afford. My father is a dedicated family man. Yet it must be confessed that my father has never hesitated to occasionally taunt the members of his family unit...

When my mother first met my father, it was in high school during a party. He was asleep on a couch the whole time. So right away she knew he was a real charmer. He has a gift for flattery, a gift that has not dissipated in their many years of marriage. In fact, not long ago, my mother asked him how he thought a pair of earrings would look with the outfit she was wearing. In his debonair manner he replied, "What, that peasant outfit? That Iranian revolutionary garb? What is that, a nurse's smock?"

My father's affection is not just limited to his family members. He had a special fondness for our late cat, Smokey. He loved to spend quality time playing with her. His favorite phrase in conjunction with Smokey was "watch what she does when I throw this at her."

My father has a great deal of generosity where his family is concerned. When my brother graduated from high school, he let him have one of the cars. We were all driving home in it one day when my brother made a left turn. The steering wheel let out a loud squeaking sound. My brother turned questioning eyes to my dad. "Do you like that?" my father asked him. "I had that feature especially installed for you so that you would know when you are turning your steering wheel too far to the left."

His generosity extends to his wife as well, of course. My mother wanted a new stove one Christmas. "Sure," he said. "I'll be glad to get you a new stove—any kind you want. Just tell me when you want to go to the store with me and pick it out." Later he told me that he would never have to buy it for her because she would ever pick it out. "She hasn't set foot in a store since we got married," he said "except for those few times when it was entirely unavoidable."

Although my father is a recluse, when it comes to family, he has few vocal reservations. If the detacher observer could see him in conversations at home, my father would appear a very different man. When he is with people he knows well, he simply loves to talk. But perhaps talk is not the proper word here. It fails to utilize the subtle nuances of the English vocabulary. I think, rather, my father s a man who loves to *inform*.

The accumulation of information has been a life-long crusade for my father. He has probably read the Bible at least five times, is well into the Random Hose Oxford Unabridged Dictionary, and has reached Volume 14 of the Funk & Wagnals encyclopedia. I once caught him murmuring something in French, a language which he has never studied, and when I asked him what he was doing, he responded, "I didn't realize this book would be written in French." Nonetheless, he went right on reading it.

It is not wise to ask my father questions, especially those you do not really want answered. Unfortunately, my father has yet to reach the r's in the Unabridged, and consequently does not know the meaning of the word rhetorical. He finds it utterly impossible to answer any question with a single word like "yes" or "no." My friend once made the mistake of asking him what road we were on as he drove us to the movies. He answered with the name of the street, but also explained who it was named after, when and where the man was born, what notable deeds he had rendered, and where his final resting place lay. Then he went on to say that several other roads in the area were named after dead men too, and of course gave extensive examples to support his claim.

Asking questions you don't want answered is a dangerous step, but when you argue with my father, you're treading on quicksand. If argument were an art, my father would be Rembrandt. It doesn't matter how much you think you know when you first get involved in an argument with him—it doesn't matter if you majored in the subject you're arguing, if you have a master's degree in it, or if you've been studying it for twenty years. My father will have some information to defend his position which you never dreamed could have existed—and he will share it with you in such a way to throw you completely off-guard. My father will then seize those precious seconds of confusion created by his unexpected thrust of information and use them to reformulate your argument so that it is in direct opposition with the facts he has acquired, even if it wasn't what you were arguing in the first place. You see, it doesn't matter what the argument was about when you began. Once my father begins to push you down that track, you could end up arguing something completely unrelated to your own beliefs. When you finally realize that you don't believe what you yourself are saying, it will be too late.

So there are two rules for dealing with my father, one about asking questions, and another forbidding argument. But there is a third and more important rule: never believe a word he says.

If my father does not know an answer to a question, he will fabricate one, and his explanations are so detailed, so realistic, and so sincerely announced that it impossible not to believe them. Usually there is little harm in such amusements…only once did my mother mistakenly teach all six of her English classes my father's illusionary story about the origin of some word. I don't recall the details, but I keenly remember my father glancing up from his book and slowly saying, You didn't."

"Yes," answered my mother. "I explained the origin to them."

"Well," my father said, "you do realize that I made that up, don't you?"

A similar deception occurred as we were searching for Davy Crockett's cabin. At last, we came across an historical marker about someone with a name resembling David Zimmerman. "That's no help," my mother said.

"Well you know," said my father, "David Zimmerman was Davy Crockett's real name. He changed it because at the time society was very anti-Semitic and he wanted to forge a name for himself on the frontier."

"Maybe we ought to go that way then," my mom suggested.

"We probably shouldn't," said my father, "considering I just made that up."

We finally did find Davy Crockett's cabin. It had been torn down and was being rebuilt to appeal to tourists. The only thing that remained was a circle of cobblestones around the area where the cabin once stood, each bearing the name of a state. My father made us walk around those cobblestones for thirty-five minutes. When I complained that the tour was slightly dull, he told me that I had absolutely no sense of history.

70

Oh, there's one more rule I forgot to mention, and this is probably the most vital—if you have any confidence in your intellectual abilities, any personal pride, and self-respect whatsoever—never—I repeat, never—challenge my father to a game of Trivial Pursuit.

"Any father who thinks he's all important should remind himself that this country honors fathers only one day a year while pickles get a whole week."
-Unknown

A Promise to St. Joseph

Jack De Vries

Adeline Sferlazza was dying. Crowded around her bed were five of her sisters, summoned to pray at the deathwatch. Adeline coughed, her lungs full of fluid and her body burning with fever. In the summer of 1922, double pneumonia was a death sentence. Adeline's physician had come three times a day during the week. Now Dr. Ring could only shake his head; there was nothing more he could do. The burial clothes were laid out, and the priest had been summoned to administer last rites. Adeline Sferlazza, who had come so far from Castellano, Sicilicy, to Passaic, New Jersey, was about to make her final journey.

Also at her bedside was my grandmother Vincenza, then sixteen years old, who was Adeline's oldest child and who was terrified of losing her mother. As she wept, she felt the hand of her Aunt Giovannina on her shoulder. "Vincenza, to save your mother, pray to St. Joseph. You are a virgin; only you can make this special vow. Promise that each year on his name day you will prepare a table in his honor. Maybe St. Joseph will spare her."

Vincenza crept into the next room. On the walls were pictures of Jesus and the Blessed Virgin. On the dresser, religious statues stood behind small, lighted candles. Vincenza knelt and prayed, pleading with St. Joseph to help her mother. She did as her aunt instructed, vowing a feast in his name for as long as she lived. "Please, St. Joseph, don't let her die," she begged.

Adeline lived through the night. She hung on the next day and through the week. Her fever cooled and her strength returned. Dr. Ring predicted that she would recover, although he did not understand why. But her family did.

That March 19th, on his name day, Vincenza began paying her debt to St. Joseph, filling the family table with a wonderful *festa*. Adeline Sferlazza helped her daughter cook, honoring the saint who had saved her. Seventy-three years later, Vincenza Sferlazza De Liberto, now 89, remains ever faithful to her vow. By saving her mother, Vincenza marked the calendar with a date that would define her family. March 19th pulls relatives and friends together like a magnet, uniting all in celebration of love, faith, and family.

The celebration of St. Joseph's Day originated in small towns in Sicily. The event was usually sponsored by the town's richest man, the *barone*. A great meal was prepared, featuring fish, vegetables, and pasta. The poor were seated in honor, with all paying homage to the patron saint of *la famiglia*, St. Joseph.

My family's story is like that of many other Sicilians. My great-grandparents, Adeline and her future husband, Emanuele, traveled by steamship to Ellis Island. They met, married, and settled in Passaic. They later moved their four children into a farmhouse at 264 Chestnut Street, complete with four rooms, a toilet on the porch, and a wood stove.

Emanuele held many jobs. He started as a barber and then switched to construction, rising to the position of foreman. His career would be a short one. While he was helping a neighbor build a garage, some iron scaffolding collapsed, and he nearly lost a leg. He would never work again. My great-grandparents had to switch roles: Adeline became the breadwinner, working by day as a weaver in the Doherty Silk Mill in Clifton. At night, she labored in her kitchen, sewing buttons on coats brought in by the rack from other factories.

In 1925, my grandmother, Vincenza, was considered a prize catch. Marriage offers were readily presented to Emanuele, who often accepted on behalf of his daughter. "Such boys," my grandmother recalled. "One had the face of a horse."

Vincenza would often go to one of her aunts for help to keep her from the altar. More help came from her mother's vivid dream in which each estranged suitor fell down a flight of stairs and then, at the end, a chubby blond man walked slowly down the same staircase. "This will be the one for my Vincenza," Adeline announced to the family. My grandfather, Joseph De Liberto, would be the one that fir the description. Along with his marriage vows, my grandfather agreed to share his bride's promise to St. Joseph.

The simple table feast grew into an event. Three days before, Adeline and Vincenza would buy cases of vegetables and begin to cook. Emanuele and his sons would remove the stuffed furniture from the house and set up long tables and benches. The neighborhood baker would prepare the bread to honor St. Joseph in the shapes of his staff, beard, halo, and cross. The smell of frying *baccala* and peppers and of simmering artichokes and lentil soup lingered over Chestnut Street.

The feast would begin with a knock on the door. "Who is it?" those inside would ask. "St. Joseph and his family," a voice would reply. The honor of playing St. Joseph would go to the neighborhood's oldest man; Mary was played by the oldest woman, and Jesus by the youngest *bambino*. "St. Joseph" was told to go away on the first two knocks, but on the third, the Holy Family would be welcomed inside. The priest would bless the food and begin the celebration.

A steady stream of people would flow into the house. First came the children from the school attended by the three De Liberto children— Sarah, Joey, and my mother, Adeline. Next came the women who worked in the sweatshops on Oak Street. At suppertime, more family neighbors, and friends would arrive. "We told everyone to come; St. Joseph would never let us run out of food," Vincenza said. And he never did.

Once, during the Depression, there was not enough money to buy St. Joseph's Day food. My grandparents prayed for help. "They took whatever money they had and bet it with a bookie on a horse," Uncle Joe remembers. "Then my mother prayed to St. Joseph." The horse won.

When their own children were grown, my grandparents brought in children from the Passaic Orphanage to replace the ones from the school. The feast grew larger when the De Liberto children brought their wives and husband's to the table.

In the early sixties, the feast moved to my Uncle Joe's home in Clifton, and by the late eighties, that house would strain to hold the gathering. One year, my cousin Rickey brought his guitar and played songs by the Rolling Stones, the Band, and the Beatles—a big departure from the traditional Italian favorites. Our music became accepted because Dee Da, as grandfather was called, thought it was "cool." Even today, fourteen years after his death, I sometimes think I can still hear his voice above the noise and music.

The holiday has since moved into a hall rented for the occasion, and this March will mark the 74th feast. Vincenza is now surrounded by her three children, ten grandchildren, nineteen great-grandchildren, and many, many friends. Old St. Joseph's Day photos show poor Italian immigrants seated at tables overflowing with food. Some of those people remain today, now old and gray. But alongside them sit their children, Italian-Americans who became teachers, doctors, nurses, artists, and entrepreneurs. Their own small children run between the tables as they did, too young to know the legacy they share. The world has changed, but the meaning of the feast—its roots in past customs, beliefs, and the love of family—remains constant.

At the head of the table, a large statue of St. Joseph looks down at the five generations of family he has blessed so often. St. Joseph rewarded Vincenza De Liberto by saving her mother and continues to reward her all the days of her life. We plan to keep my grandmother's vow long after she is gone. I hope St. Joseph will be as kind to us as he has been to generations past.

From *New Jersey Monthly*, March 1996

"This is the true joy in life, the being used for a purpose recognized by yourself as a mighty one; the being a force of nature instead of a feverish, selfish little cold of ailments and grievances that the world will not devote itself to making you happy."
-George Bernard Shaw

Bubbe and Zayde Wasserman

Remembering Bubbe

Sherri Waas Shunfenthal

Remembering Bubbe is like sifting through a scrapbook of memories. I don't have a single picture, but many pictures and stories gleaned from many sources. Scattered memories come from stories told by my mother, her siblings, my own memories and photographs. Some of my memories have dimmed. My time with my Bubbe was short. She died when I was eight. My memories as well as stories told by my mother and her siblings form the fabric and texture of who I am. Bubbe's soul is part of me.

Stories about her have been kept alive by the wonderful stories my relatives tell. These stories help to form the fabric and texture of who I am.

Bubbe and Zayde had an extraordinary love. They met in their native Rumania. Deeply in love, they secretly sneaked into the village graveyard (the only place Bubbe and Zayde could have privacy) to talk quietly or exchange a kiss. Bubbe's grandfather was a rabbi and her family was wealthy because they owned land. Zayde's family was poor and did not own land. Bubbe and Zayde desperately wanted to marry. Bubbe's family did not approve. At 18, however, Bubbe's love won out.

My scrapbook does not have details on how Bubbe was able to convince her parents that she should marry Zayde. They married and bravely left Rumania and their families to travel to the land of promise, America. Zayde's family was no longer safe in Rumania because one of Zayde's relatives killed a Russian soldier during a pogrom. A pogrom was when Russian soldiers swept through a village and massacre the Jewish villagers. They randomly slaughtered families.

Though times were difficult, I try to imagine leaving family and friends, being a young bride on a ship traveling to a new country. Bubbe did not know English and did not have t.v to show her pictures of America. The only image she had in her head was from my Zayde's relative's letters or from Zayde's dream of moving to a better place. It was probably more difficult for Bubbe since she came from a wealthier family and had more comforts in life. They were able to take very little with them.

I moved from Philadelphia to California when I married. I knew the language and still it was difficult. I cannot imagine being 18, leaving everyone I grew up with behind and going to an unseen new world.

Together Bubbe and Zayde embarked on an incredible journey to a new land, America. I wonder how my Bubbe felt as she traveled to America. Was she full of hope and destiny? Was she fearful or terrified? Was she so much in love with Zayde that she followed him on this adventure not thinking of the hardships she might endure? Was it a love filled with promise, a new land, a new people? I can only imagine that their great love for each other and my Zayde's enthusiasm helped them on this journey.

I traveled once on a weekend cruise ship and was nauseous the whole time because we hit some rough water. Bubbe and Zayde traveled simply in steerage for weeks. A hard bed, a bathroom to share with others, a tiny space. Bubbe had only some dishes, some silver, clothing and her feather pillows. Was this enough to remind Bubbe of home? Did Bubbe get sick on this long journey? Was she sick at heart to leave her family? The answers elude me. I cannot imagine such a long journey. Was Bubbe seasick or filled with eager anticipation? My scrapbook does not answer my questions. My aunts told me Bubbe rarely told her emotions.

A relative of Zayde's sponsored my grandparent's coming to America. Bubbe and Zayde initially lived with these relatives. Bubbe had never met them before. What could it have been like for Bubbe, a stranger, living in a distant relative's home? She did not speak English but they probably were able to speak Yiddish with her. Zayde got work right away selling fruit from a fruit stand. Bubbe had no place of her own. Most of the money Zayde earned was saved to bring Zayde's relatives to America.

Bubbe became pregnant in the new land. What was it like for her to bear children at such a young age - 19 or 20, with no mother by her side to give advice or help? I depend so much on my mother's counsel.

What was it like for Bubbe all alone? My mother tells me that all Bubbe's pregnancies were difficult. She had miscarriages that she would not talk about. She did give birth to and raised five healthy children. When my Uncle Jack was born, he weighed only two pounds. Zayde came to the hospital excited to see his newborn son but when he saw one so tiny, he felt sick. Uncle Jack was so tiny that Bubbe and Zayde brought him home in a breadbasket. It was a true miracle that Jack survived without medical aid but he was fed love and milk and grew to be one of Bubbe and Zayde's tallest children. He also turned out to be the most mischievous, active child and caused his parents the most trouble!

My aunts tell me that Bubbe did not complain or talk about her fears aloud. She must have been frightened during each pregnancy. Did she hover over Uncle Jack who was so small? What must he have looked like so wrinkled and miniature? I wish I knew Bubbe and Zayde's feelings and thoughts. My own mother was only four pounds at birth. Bubbe must have feared for her tiny newborns.

My uncles say Zayde adapted more easily to America than Bubbe. He began life in America selling from a fruit pushcart, then a fruit stand, until he eventually could buy a store of his own. He picked up English fairly easily. Zayde was a hard worker, smart and scrupulously honest. He had a great sense of humor and a zest for life. He used to tease his children, "If you find a dollar, you must find who it belongs to immediately and give it back for they will need it. If you find a thousand dollars, you can keep it because anyone who can lose a thousands dollars can manage to do without it." Zayde saved every cent he earned. He and Bubbe managed to send for Zayde's parents and siblings to come live in America.

My aunts tell stories about Bubbe's stamina and endurance. She helped Zayde in the store, worked long hours by his side, even on weekends. She was respectful and kind to everyone. The customers loved Bubbe's gentle nature. In addition to the long hours in the store she managed to raise the kids, cook and clean. I remember Bubbe telling me once, "I do what I need to do." If something had to be done, she had only herself and Zayde to rely on. Bubbe made the choice to embrace life, do what she needed and not resent hard work.

In 1932, Bubbe and Zayde tried to make a return visit to Rumania. How Bubbe missed her family and longed to hold them in her vision. How excited Bubbe must have been! Mom tells me how Bubbe longed to see her family so she could carry back with her the memories.

Bubbe and Zayde reached Paris by boat. In Paris, the authorities told Bubbe she was still considered a citizen of Rumania. If she went to Rumania, they might not let her out again. Laws had changed in America and Bubbe had not automatically become an American citizen when Zayde was naturalized. Bubbe's heart must have broken! She and Zayde had saved for this trip and traveled so far. Now they had to journey home without seeing Bubbe's family. How did she live with the sorrow?

Soon after Bubbe and Zayde returned to America, Bubbe became a naturalized citizen of the United States and they began to save again to travel to Rumania. In 1934, they were able to make that trip. This time they arrived. The whole village turned out to greet Bubbe and Zayde as if they were royalty! It was Bubbe's day to be Queen.

When Bubbe returned to America she relayed to her children the wonder of it. Bubbe must have enjoyed every moment of that visit.

79

How I wish I had her here now to hear the details of her family so I might know them in some way. After 1937, Bubbe never received any more letters. She never heard from any of her relatives again. They all perished in the Holocaust.

Years later, my mother read an account of Bubbe's home village. The Jewish villagers were forced into the local synagogue and burned to death by Nazi soldiers and their local helpers. A whole town vanished.

What must Bubbe have felt after the war to know her whole family, friends and village were erased like a like a mark on a paper? Did she carry this thought in her head each day of the rest of her life? Mom tells me Bubbe rarely spoke of her personal feelings but after the war Bubbe guarded her children possessively. Perhaps she feared for them or worried that they too could vanish. Her children and her husband were the only immediate family she had. Her own parents, siblings, aunts, uncles, cousins and childhood friends were all gone.

Bubbe was not demonstrative yet her children knew she would gladly lay her life down for them. Her children knew she loved them deeply. I remember Bubbe's beautiful clear, brown eyes. When I looked into her eyes, I could feel her love. Bubbe rarely kissed me, yet when I felt her gentle brown eyes upon me, it felt as if she was touching me. And when she would smile at me, I felt special.

I remember in Bubbe's later years when mom and I would visit her. We'd sit on Bubbe's bed and watch the tv show, Queen for a Day. Bubbe loved that show. Perhaps she dreamed of winning something special or being Queen for one Day. But to me she was like a queen and I just love sitting next to her on the bed, feeling close to her and being in her company. There was a feeling of gentle strength that radiated from her.

Each of my relatives gave me a sentence that described Bubbe. "She took care of us children and her husband, worked long hours in the store, cooked, cleaned and never complained." "She never said a mean word about anyone and would not let any of her children say an unkind word to anyone." My Aunt told me that though Bubbe did not speak English well but she told her children, "If you have a mouth, use it. If you need help, ask for it." "She had a soft, gentle soul but she was strong and always did what needed to be done." Most of all, "She put her family's needs above her own."

To me, Bubbe was like all the cherished women of the Bible. She was like Ruth who was a kind, good friend, a good wife and did what needed to be done without complaint or bitterness. Bubbe was like Rebekkah who journeyed from her home to be with her husband. She was like Esther who was beautiful inside and out. She also had courage to come to a new world and by so doing helped to save a generation.

Near the end of her life Bubbe was very ill and in a nursing home but she turned to my mother and said out of compassion, "It must be so hard for you to see your mother here." She also had a sense of humor. One day my Aunt and my mother came to visit Bubbe but she was sleeping when they arrived. My mother and Aunt started talking to each other. Bubbe woke up and said, "Oy, oy, it's so noisy in here!" "But mom, my mother said, "only Natalie and I are here." "I know," Bubbe said. "All that noise is coming from your mouth!"

On the day before she died, Bubbe opened her eyes wide, looked at mom, and told her, "Time passes like a fly in the night, Sylvia."

Time passes too quickly, Bubbe. I wish you were here to talk with and to embrace you in a hug. Sometimes we do not realize how significant a person's story is until they are gone. If you had not followed Zayde to America, Bubbe, I would not be here today. I might never have been born or might have perished in the Holocaust like all of your relatives. Thank you for your courage.

I take my scrapbook and turn the pages, Bubbe. The stories I have heard about you have shaped my life. My mother and her siblings have conveyed the essence of you in their stories. I am filled with admiration for you and glad to be your granddaughter. Your bravery, your compassion, your spirit are part of me. I may not have you here with me but I have some of your stories. I feel the love that you had for your children and the incredible love they had for you. I will remember. I remember Bubbe.

In loving memory of Clara and Sam Wasserman.

"The real measure of life is not its duration, but its donation."
-Corrie Ten Boom

NOTE: Bubbe means "grandmother" and Zayde means "grandfather" in Yiddish.

As I Saw It

Sylvia Douet

BLACKMAN & SONS, MASTER FISHMONGER & POULTERER, the sign painted in black letters on a brown background was a proud statement by Syd Blackman when he moved his family to a residential neighbourhood in the late 1920's. This was where he would prosper, perhaps one of the boys would be happy to take over the shop when the time came for him to retire, and they would go into business together, so life would be easier all round. He had survived the war, unlike his brother Frank, who had been killed in Europe. It had been quite exciting in the Flying Core, and Syd felt very lucky to have married Annie, his sweetheart, and here they were in Richings Park with their children.

Richings Park was a new estate which had been built to serve the upwardly mobile families of the district, and the estate was part of Iver, which included Iver Heath, where the Duchess of Kent had a home, and also the Mosley family.

The residents of the estate were mainly business men, married with families, who took the train into the City of London, about twenty miles away, each morning to work. The men wore bowler hats, and carried long rolled umbrellas as a mark of their position.

The trains stopped at Iver station, in Richings Park. The railway line ran from Paddington Station in London, via Iver, then on to Langley and Slough, and sometimes going on to Windsor. It was a big event when the Royal Train was passing through, on its way to Windsor, when the royals went to stay at Windsor Castle. The Union Jacks were brought out, and the children would peer threw the bedroom windows, from where they could see the trains passing, hoping to get a glimpse of the King or Queen, or even little Princess Elizabeth or Margaret. A great favourite of the children was standing on the railway bridge as the trains went through and inhaling the smoke from the engines.

There was a large Manor House in Richings Park, which_was surrounded by acres of land, with many stately old trees. There were several streets with detached houses, and the shopping area.

Syd's shop was one of a row of eight, including the Butcher, the Baker, the Chemist, and the Dairy. The other shops in the area were two Grocery stores, two Stationers where the papers were sold, and also jars of sweets, and chocolate bars, a Bank, and the Haberdasher, an old fashioned store with shelves piled high with boxes of underwear, socks, linens, and some dresses and hats in all sizes and colors, from frilly to plain, to suit all tastes. This was a busy store as the nearest competition would be by train about eight miles away. The stores were all unique in their set-up, especially the Fish-shop which had a marble slab to display the fish on. The fish was kept fresh by constant spraying with fresh water and ice packed around it. Supplies were kept fresh in the ice-box, as there was no electric refrigerator, only a supply of large slabs of ice delivered by the Iceman. Electricity was available for lighting but it was too costly for refrigeration.

There was no reason that the store should not prosper, but often the bills were slow in being paid, and with a family to feed it was not always easy for Syd. It was especially irksome when it was expected that the Fishmonger should raise his hat as a mark of respect to his customers.

Syd felt life was good. Tiring at times, but with Annie by his side, all would be well.

With another child on the way, Kathleen would be a great help, especially since the Doctor had told them after the last birth, that another pregnancy would be difficult for Annie. Syd felt that Audrey was a bit of a dreamer, but Beryl was a capable girl. Cliff would be leaving school soon, and Des could run the errands. Ron and Sylv weren't babies anymore, they were just 'nippers' though, as his Cockney upbringing thought of them.

Christmas 1936 was a happy one. The tree was put up on Christmas eve by the older children, with Audrey dressed as Santa Claus. "Sh!Sh! Sh!" they said at the top of their voices. It was such fun they almost woke the younger children, who were almost too excited to sleep. The little ones woke to Christmas morning to find a pillow-case on their beds filled with toys and candies, perhaps a little shop with jars of candies, or a book was a treasured gift, hard to believe that Santa Claus had been and that they had missed him. It was an unwritten rule that nobody moved on Christmas morning until they heard the adults up and about. They played with their toys in bed or ate the candies and oranges, they had found in their pillow case. Now it was time for the little ones to hush their voices, as Mum and Dad were sleeping.

The days before had been filled with preparing turkeys, geese and ducks for Christmas dinners. The shop had been hung with poultry, all of which had been prepared by Syd and his helpers. Everyone was tired, as even the older children were expected to help pluck the feathers from the birds, which had to be cleaned and singed and dressed before sale.

Annie and the girls prepared the goose for dinner. The smell of the sage, in the stuffing drove everyone mad, and excited at the thought of eating this bird a few hours away. The Christmas cake had been made weeks before, and the plum pudding, which had several sixpences put in for the lucky person on Christmas Day was steaming in the pot on the stove. The children who were free from chores, were allowed to go to the Sitting-room, where a coal fire was burning for the one day of the year. The phonograph was played. It was operated by hand, and one of the favourite songs was "Boiled Beef and Carrots", the sound coming from the horn. The children read books, or played with their new Christmas presents, so when Mum and Dad joined them they enjoyed some Tizer or Ginger Beer, had Figs or Dates which were a real treat. Dad had a shot of Brandy with Soda from the syphon. The candles were lit on the tree, where they sat on little candle holders which were clipped onto the tree, and which collected the wax as it ran, only burning for a short while as everyone watched in fascination.. The children played "Hunt the Thimble," or "I Spy". Christmas Dinner was ready at about three o'clock, and it was a great feast so that everyone ate too much, enjoyed pulling the Christmas Crackers and wore silly paper hats. Steaming Christmas Pudding saturated with brandy was brought by Dad flaming to the table. There was no thought of any more food that day except a piece of Cake at bedtime with a cup of cocoa. Christmas passed and it was time for the baby to be born on January 1 1937.

ANNIE FRANCIS

"Let me see" demanded the six year old girl. "Is this our baby? I'm going to ask Mum! Where is she?". Sylvia had been surprised to find a baby basket in the kitchen. The house was unusually quiet, and she couldn't find Mum. Granny had come to help with the family of five girls and three boys, while Dad was still busy in the fish-shop, preparing orders for the customers who still expected service, most of them unaware of the death in the family. The children were told not to go into the big bedroom, but it wasn't long before they had to peep, and discover a long box, but were afraid to look again. Their comprehension of death was unreal. Why did Mum have to go away?, and this new baby was just like a doll, but seemed to need so much attention.

"I'm going to Betty's house". Unable to understand what was happening to her world, the hush instead of constant activity that a large family makes, Sylvia was uncomfortable, not understanding that this death would change life for all of them.

Betty was very happy to see her. They played in the large sandbox in the garden of the detached house where Betty lived. There was no snow, otherwise they could have tobogganed on the hill nearby.

Betty's mother made sandwiches for lunch and was especially kind to the fishmonger's little girl. She wondered what would happen to this family? How would the father manage with eight surviving children? Probably they would go to St Bernardo's Homes where they would at least have a roof over their heads.

The children continued to play, but Sylvia was still upset by the changes at home, and she demanded to play with Betty's favourite doll, because as she told Betty "My Mum just died". Betty an only child couldn't possibly understand.

Monday came and the big box was taken out of the house, with much hushing and the children told to be quiet, and to keep out of the way. Granny came back again afterwards, and everyone had tea. Dad was very sad, and the children understood that Mum had gone to heaven.

Sydney Blackman in his early forties, was devastated. His Annie was gone. How could he carry on with this family?. It was hard enough working in the cold fish-shop from six o'clock in the morning, sometimes until eleven o'clock at night. There were orders to prepare, fish to fillet, salmon to smoke, fish-cakes to make, and pleasing the customers.

Kathleen at only seventeen would have her hands full with a house to run, and a new baby as well. As he climbed the stairs to his home without the wonderful wife that Annie had been, he worried whether she would be able to look after the other children properly, Annie had been a great cook (she had learned at the Nursing Home in Hayes where she had been in service before they married).Annie had made the girls dresses, and together they had managed when things were tight. Syd was well able to repair the shoes when they became worn, and cutting their hair was a pleasure to keep them looking neat and tidy. He told himself that he would carry on for Annie's sake, and would call the baby Annie after her mother, hoping that she would grow up with the same kind nature.

Life to the six year old Sylvia seemed just the same, except that now it was Kathleen who took care of everything instead of Mum. At seventeen, Kathleen now had a family of nine to look after, in a two bedroom flat over the store. There were no modern facilities. Laundry was washed in the kitchen sink, rinsed in the bath-tub, then put through the rollers of the mangle, which sat permanently on the end of the bath-tub, to remove the excess water. The challenge then was in drying the clothes, when possible on the line in the back-yard, but on wet days lines were strung across the kitchen and the clothes hung there. Fortunately the bedding was sent out, but with small children and the inevitable wet beds, this would have been a problem. The kitchen was the hub of the house, heated with a range which burned coke, (a substance derived from coal,) and this in turn heated the hot water tank which was in a cupboard where the clothes would be aired after washing and ironing. The range could also be used for cooking, but there was an electric stove and kettle.

It is hard to imagine this room now, it was big enough to have a large kitchen table, where all the meals were eaten, also the large pantry for storing the foods, a sideboard for the dishes and cutlery, besides the range and stove. The kitchen was used for many other things as it was the only warm room in the house. This included sewing on the old Singer treadle machine, homework from school, and on Sunday nights Syd would be seen doing his accounts for the shop. Since Television was not known in those days, the radio was a great favourite, especially at five o' clock when children's hour came on and stories were told.

Kathleen had a Beau at this time, and his name was Laurie. He would come to help Syd in the shop, and also would help Kathleen play with the children before putting them to bed.

One Sunday everyone had to be especially clean because a lady by the name of Miss Brown was coming to dinner. The Vicar of the Anglican Church had arranged for her to come and visit, to see whether she might take the position of housekeeper.

Soon she had moved in. Kathleen and Audrey the two eldest girls went to live with Auntie Grace, their mother's sister, leaving eight people in the flat. Miss Brown was given the living room with a pull out couch for sleeping, and in other homes it would have been called the parlour, it was the best room in the flat, and in those days was only used about once a year, at Christmas, or for very special occasions. It was highly polished, dusted regularly, and contained the piano and bookcases. The rest of the family shared the other two bedrooms.

Miss Brown quickly got the family organized. It seemed that there was little she could not do, and everyone was expected to work along with her. The front stairs had to be swept from top to bottom and the front entrance way washed every morning before breakfast and school. Saturday morning was time to wash the kitchen floor, dust the house and polish the sitting room, besides helping Dad with delivery of orders and other chores. Everyone was expected to excel at school and at home. The efficiency was great, but there was no love shown and the children were under great tension from missing their mother's love, and not sure when a heavy hand would descend upon them. Syd, busy in the shop, was unaware of the unhappiness in the family, so he felt very relieved that the family was receiving care.

Meals were very different in those days. Breakfast was always a cooked meal. Sausages with fried bread, herrings or bloaters (like a herring but smoked), fish-cakes, fish roes, or sometimes a piece of smoked cod or haddock. Dinner was served at noon, and on a week-day might be rabbit stew, or tripe (not a favourite). Living next to the butcher was an advantage as he would put cheap cuts aside for Syd's family, but on Sundays a roast was usually served. The children all went to Iver school about a mile away, and they all came home for dinner. Tea was a favourite meal, at about five o'clock, mostly consisting of bread and jam, a pot of tea, and if they were lucky a piece of fruit cake. At bedtime another piece of bread and jam, and a cup of cocoa. The bread was always fresh as the bakeshop was just a few stores away, and sometimes a slice of Hovis bread was a special treat.

Bedtime was an ordeal to be endured in the winter as the bedrooms were cold and also the beds, so it was a routine to roll oneself into a ball until you fell asleep and the body heat took over. Sylvia loved to read in bed, so she would find a flashlight, and hide with it under the covers, hoping not to get caught.

Annie was very much loved by everyone as she grew into a toddler, and Miss Brown became her mother in every sense of the word. She loved her as if she were her own. She also took seriously her position in the family by helping Clifford to become apprenticed as a toolmaker as soon as he left school at the age of fourteen, followed by Desmond a couple of years later.

On Mondays the shop was closed, giving Syd a chance to catch up on filleting or curing the fish, or cooking for making fish-cakes. When possible he took the train into Slough to shop or perhaps to see the barber for a haircut or for advice on how to preserve the little hair he had left. He was relieved that the housekeeper had worked out so well. She was a smart woman, and knew how to run the household, relieving him of a great deal of worry. It was good to have an adult to talk with, and , she seemed to enjoy talking to him as well. Considering her background it was quite surprising.

Sylvia Brown had been born of well to do parents, and had lived a comfortable and well educated life with her family. At twenty-one she had been engaged to be married, but her fiancee had been killed in a motorcycle accident. It was rumoured that she had been sent on a world tour, but on returning her life had seemed empty, so she had accepted the position of housekeeper to the Blackman family.

Suddenly the children were told to call Miss Brown "Auntie". It was hard to change a habit they had developed, but Dad seemed to be angry when the children persisted in calling her Miss Brown. In time the change was made, and there were rumours that Dad and Auntie were married. Apart from this life went on just the same with it's daily routine of chores and responsibilities. Auntie was difficult to please, and Ronald was often in trouble because of his mischievous nature. The older children were all employed. Kathleen was employed as a telephonist at the local Post-office, Audrey worked at the Fairey Aviation Company as a secretary, and Beryl was apprenticed with a dress-maker.

WW 2

October 1939 the second world war was declared, and this made more serious changes to their lives. An air-raid shelter was built in the back-yard, this was no small feat since the yard was very small. It was never used as an air-raid shelter because it was very damp and cold. When the bombing came too close, Syd would carry the children to the cupboard under the stairs. Every-one was expected to carry a Gas-mask, a horrible rubber thing with plastic windows for the eyes, and made to fit snugly so that no gas would penetrate. There were practices for using it, but it had a horrible rubber smell which was not appreciated. The store next to the fish shop was turned into an emergency headquarters.

Sirens became an everyday occurence, and although Iver was about twenty miles from London, there were some close calls, such as a landmine in the local park. In the later part of the war there were "Doodle Bugs" otherwise known as the Flying bombs which looked like a plane flying over, but was pilotless and made a horrible droning noise until the engine stopped, when hopefully it wasn't overhead, as at this time it would fall to earth and explode, causing death and destruction. The citizens hoped the Flying Bomb would be shot down before this happened.

Kathleen became engaged to Laurie, and her wedding was planned to be held in April 1940 at the Anglican Church in West-Drayton. Auntie Grace, who Kathleen was living with, arranged the wedding, and made all the dresses. She was a tailoress by profession, so every-one looked lovely, from the bride in white, to the three little bridesmaids, cousin Pamela, Sylvia and Annie who was a little small to appreciate all the fuss.

Syd joined the Home Guard. Too old to be enlisted in the forces, he was determined to do his bit at home. The men patrolled the area, in Home Guard uniform, and were available when emergencies struck. Food rationing was enforced to help to keep supplies of food available for everyone. There were ration books containing coupons showing what entitlement each individual had, depending on the age and nutritional needs, and food was bought from the stores accordingly. Being in the food business was a little help as the store keepers would be the first to know when supplies came in, but nobody was getting fat. The local recreation field was turned into an allotment for families to grow their own vegetables. Business in the shop was slow because of shortages, caused by the risk to fishermen due to the war, so Syd took a job in a munitions factory in Slough. He was mechanically inclined and enjoyed this part-time work.

Auntie appeared to be in her element, and started teaching cooking classes, and also as an accomplished seamstress, making clothes for some of the people in the area, such as Lady Mosley or The Duchess of Kent. She was also employed as a Cutter for the clothing factory which had sprung up in the old movie theatre, which had closed at the beginning of the war.

The children who were still at home were expected to do their bit. Summer jobs included working on farms, helping with the hay-baling, sorting potatoes, or picking tomatoes in a green-house. They also had membership in brownies, girl guides, scouts or cubs, and when necessary had to deliver fish to the houses on the tradesman's bicycle, which had a large basket on the front for the orders. These orders were often phoned into the store, and if Dad was busy the one of the children would answer "Iver 203". A simple number compared to modern times. The telephone, the old-fashioned kind had a black pedestal base and a separate hand piece. The telephone was there strictly for business, and since the children had no friends with telephones it was a novelty to answer the phone in the shop.

The war effort was on everyone's mind, and there were displays such as a German plane which had been shot down, in the old cinema parking lot. The idea was to save money for the war effort, so a line of pennies was collected until a target amount had been saved. A similar effort was put on when a barrage balloon was on display in the local recreation field.

As soon as Cliff was old enough he volunteered for the Royal Air Force. Audrey, and later Beryl joined the Women's Auxillary Army Corp's or W.A.A.C.'s as it was called, and then it was Desmond's turn, and he joined the Royal Navy.

Cliff was soon was off to Canada as a pilot trainee. Eventually he became a Pilot Officer flying Spitfires, but the memory that Sylvia had of him, was the delicious chocolate he brought back from Canada, in this time of deprivation. Desmond became a Petty Officer in the Royal Navy, and again Sylvia was happy to receive nylon stockings from him, as they were so scarce, and she was by then starting to grow up. Beryl went to Paris as a part of S.H.A.E.F. and Audrey was to marry a Canadian Merchant Marine, emigrating to Canada as a War-bride, with her baby Paula.

Friday was the day when Syd Blackman sold 'Fish & Chips, the remainder of the week was for fresh fish sales.

On Fridays in the 1940's, when Sylvia was about twelve years old, she would arrive home from school in her navy tunic & blouse with tie, and the rest of her day was used to help Dad in the shop.

Answering the telephone "Iver 203." "Just a minute and I will get Mr Blackman." "Dad! Mrs Jones wants some fish and chips"

After changing into her old skirt and sweater, she would go into the small room with the large sink, where the potatoes were being scrubbed. Picking up a bowl full of potatoes she went to the chip cutter.

"Make sure that you put the potato in upright, Sylv, or you'll pinch your fingers, and when you are finished give them here, so that I can put them in the fryer," said Dad.

Dad was wearing a brown overall coat, covered with a large white apron. The room was at the back of the downstairs, behind the main fish shop. There was a large window, with the light coming in, but it was one of those dull overcast days, so Syd needed the light on to see the fish and chip frying pans. They were two deep fryers, filled with oil, and brought to a high temperature to make the fish batter crisp. The batter was in a large bowl. "How smooth this is today," thought Syd, as he dipped the Hake into the batter, drawing it out quickly so that a thin crisp batter on the fish would be edible.

"Dad! I can't cut this one, it's too big" said Sylvia. "O.K. you little hussy, let me give a hand," was Dad's fond reply.

"Mrs Jones wants two pieces of Hake, one piece of Sole, and six pen'uth of chips." "I oiled the bike so it's in good shape. Just deliver this to her right away." "She lives at 12 Syke Ings, and go to the back door."

While he was talking, he took the freshly cooked fish, and drained it in a wire basket, also the chips in another basket, then placed them on two pieces of greaseproof paper and wrapped them. Finally wrapping them in newspaper, which kept them warm, writing the address and cost on the corner of the paper, perhaps a little malt vinegar and salt might be added later.(Even now you might find an Englishman riding on a bus eating his fish and chips, perhaps after a movie or on his way home from work.)

Sylvia put the package into the basket of the bike. The bike was a trades bike, meant for a man to ride with a bar across, with a trades basket about eighteen inches deep on the front. It was no problem for Sylvia to ride this bike, as she had learned to ride on her brother's bike at age five, and at twelve years old she was now quite used to cocking her leg over the seat. Bicycle riding was the main form of transportation around the estate, and the children all learned early.

Sylvia went to the house, it wasn't far, just around the corner on the next street, but it was dark and Mrs Jones had forgotten to put the light on. She hoped that no-one would pop their head around from behind the hedge, as she made her way to the door.

"Thank-you Sylvia, that was quick" said Mrs Jones as she opened the door. She was quite tall, with red hair, and a friendly smile. "We are really looking forward to our supper. I look forward to Friday night's Fish and Chips." "How much is that?" "Two shillings and sixpence? Well here's another tuppence for you."

Riding home was a bit cool, as it was November, so Sylvia rode quickly looking forward to her own fish and chips that Dad had promised.

Feeling good, Sylvia took her package of fish and chips and climbed the backstairs to the kitchen. As she sat down, Auntie came into the room. "You had better hurry up eating that. I presume you have homework to do.?"

"Yes" was the mumbled reply, out of a mouth full of chips.

"Well, before you do that, you can wash the dishes, and you didn't dust the front room properly, so there is that to do as well."

It was already six o'clock, so Sylvia said "There isn't time to do my homework and the dishes."

"I can't help that," said Auntie "You'll do them anyway, and don't come whining to me if it's not done."

"How can I get it all done?" complained Sylvia, in a desperate voice, but children in the 1940's did not argue with parents or guardians.

The local school was in the village of Iver, which all of the Blackman children attended, usually until the age of fourteen. It was then expected that they would become apprenticed to learn a trade or find a job. The other alternative was to pass a scholarship to go to high school at the age of ten or eleven years, otherwise another scholarship was offered for a comprehensive school at age thirteen which concentrated on more practical subjects for job placement.

Annie passed the scholarship at ten years of age, and Sylvia at eleven, presumably because of the influence of Auntie who pushed them hard to study. When Sylvia went to high school it was like a dream come true, nobody in the family had this opportunity before, and to learn French was so exciting. The first year went well and Sylvia excelled enough to be placed with the top line in her year.

The second year was much more difficult and struggling to keep up the grades was very difficult, so that when her marks were not enough to please Auntie, Sylvia became discouraged, and as she was also a day dreamer when it was time for homework, assignments were not completed, and detentions would be sent home. Occasionally Dad would sign these detentions but going to Auntie would be more than she could bear, so Sylvia would perform a little forgery and hope to get away with it.

After the first year of challenge, and with Latin on the agenda, which she never understood, life became more difficult. Tensions at home gave her little incentive to achieve, and because she was a reclusive child it was difficult for her to explain her feelings. Auntie couldn't understand why she couldn't get higher grades, so by fourteen she couldn't wait to leave home.

What could she possibly do, with another two years before leaving school?

At this time Sylvia developed a spot on her instep. Then there was a redness in her groin, and finally she told Auntie who was naturally very cross that she hadn't mentioned it sooner, and took her to the doctor. She was operated on for an abscess in her right groin. Three weeks and many injections later Sylvia returned home but with a different outlook on life, as it was an experience she wouldn't forget in a hurry. She had been cared for in a different way, and although she had been ill, it had been rather pleasant. She began to think about being a nurse, and was encouraged because this looked like the answer to leaving home. At fifteen she joined the red Cross. Relatives were shocked that this skinny girl should want to be a nurse, feeling that she would not be strong enough.

School holidays were spent working at the local hospital, where she enjoyed taking temperatures, even though she was teased by the patients because she took everything so seriously. She had a small pulsometer (somewhat like an egg-timer) which ran for half a minute for counting pulses, and would gaze seriously at this while holding the patients wrist . She was very proud of the Red Cross uniform. A blue dress and white apron with the large red cross on it. A white headpiece, like a large starched scarf pulled tightly around her head, and fanned out at the back. For a fifteen year old it was very exciting, and perhaps she had found her niche.

"The family is one of nature's masterpieces."
-George Santayana

Years

Carol Sue Hair

The wind carries with it all the years --
the centuries gone by
Billowing wide the sails of ships transporting courage
Rushing cold through valleys rimmed all round
by the unknown
Blasting sere across the summer prairies
Sighing soft by streams awash in silver mist

The wind carries with it echoes of old stories --
the past that is our own
The echoes of Love made and Tears shed
Child born and Cannon fired
Hunger stifled and Valor tried
Prayers mumbled and Laughter shared
Passings mourned and mourned again

The wind touches all with force or tenderness
We feel the ancient ice and heat of it
We take within our souls the sounds it brings
We listen to the years
And remember

The wind moves on--burdened anew
with echoes of the present
Adding to its store of whispers from the past
But it leaves a precious gift within the heart
The knowledge sure that Death *cannot* exist

    While the wind lives
        and there is someone
                who will listen to the years
                and not forget

Contributors

MICHAEL D. ARNOLD lives in Manassas, Virginia, with his wife Valerie, a dog, and two cats. He is originally from Mansfield, Louisiana, but relocated to Virginia after receiving an Honorable Discharge from the United States Air Force. He is currently in school to receive a degree in Art and has contributed art work to several books. He took a break from paint and brush, to test his skills at writing.

SKYLAR HAMILTON BURRIS was born in Northern Virginia and attended the University of Virginia in Charlottesville, where she earned her BA in English and Economics. She also earned a Master's in English from the University of Texas at Brownsville. She is the editor of her own home press magazine, *Ancient Paths*, and has had her work published in several magazines, including *Aim*, *The Lyric*, *Time of Singing*, and *Raconteur*.

RONALD RODGER CASEBY was born in Scotland in 1936 and was the sixth and last child of the Rev. Alexander and Williamina Caseby. In his formative years, parental love and the encouragement of learning were as bountiful in our ever happy household as money and material possessions were scarce. Since retiring early in 1993 from careers in Personal Management and College Lecturing, he has occupied his spare time researching and writing about the genealogy of his family. For more, see his page on RootsWeb.

PATTY COLOMBE is a 35-year-old registered nurse, born and raised in a small outpost in Newfoundland, Canada. The people of this community, especially her family, are very colorful and full of fun. Despite living in a slow paced environment, many interesting things happen. Some are not easily explained. We don't think about these unexplainable things much...only when they happen (which is almost daily). It would have been a great place for Rod Serling or E. A. Poe.

JACK De VRIES began his writing career in 1991 by winning Bloomfield College's George M. Jones Award for literary excellence. His first published work appeared in the 1991 Cleveland Indians Yearbook, and he has written for the Indians ever since. Jack also has written numerous stories for the *USA Today Baseball Weekly*, *Beckett Tribute*, and *New Jersey Monthly Magazine*, and authors a weekly column on sports for New Jersey's *Herald & News*.

ESTHER DiLUCA, a native of Lexington, Massachusetts, now resides in Reading. A graduate of Burdett College, she worked in the secretarial field for several years. Esther has one daughter. After returning to the business world, she became interested in evening classes at the Middlesex Community College where she studied many selected subjects including poetry and writing. Esther is a member of The Writer's Club at the MITRE Corporation in Bedford, Massachusetts.

SYLVIA DOUET started writing memoirs about five years ago when she was learning to use a computer. In November of 1999, she took a Life Writing Course in St. Catherines, Ontario, Canada with Mae Denby as her teacher, as part of an Elder Hostel program.

Hailing from Kansas, LELA EITEL considers family her first priority and is rightfully proud of her children. As a 25th Anniversary gift, her children sent her and her husband on a whirlwind tour of Europe. There they visited ancestral villages, the bright lights of Paris, Heidelberg, and numerous castle ruins. In Italy, they saw the Pope. Lela's pastimes include genealogy, travel, gardening, and reading.

RUSTY FISCHER is a former teacher who now writes for a small publisher in Orlando, Florida. His writing has appeared in numerous national publications and he has been anthologized in the *Chicken Soup for the Soul* books, *A Gift of Miracles*, and *More God's Abundance*. He is married to another former teacher and together he and his wife Martha enjoy traveling, walking, dining out, and going to movies. He still calls his grandmother once a week.

In retirement, V. ARLENE WOODHOUSE FRODEY enjoys researching her family and learning about the lives of her ancestors. She also enjoys travel and nature photography with her husband Ray. Their stories and photography have been published in several local papers.

CAROLSUE HAIR is a published author and working editor, born in Norman, Oklahoma in 1944. She is currently researching and editing a history of the 27th Infantry in the Vietnam War, *The Wolfhounds in Vietnam – Brothers in Blood*, being written by H.L. "Dutch" McAllister, Major, US Army, Retired. She is employed full time by NBC Internet as a technical support agent.

J. THOMAS HETRICK edits this volume. He's the author two books covering 19th century baseball history. His second book, *Chris Von der Ahe and the St. Louis Browns*, was a Finalist for the Seymour Medal in 2000, given the best book of baseball history or biography the previous year. Hetrick also owns and operates Pocol Press, a vibrant publisher in Clifton, Virginia.

Thirty nine-year-old DORIA DEE JOHNSON was born in Evanston, Illinois. She currently lives in Washington, DC and works as a freelance writer. She hope to turn her story into a documentary or full-length feature film.

CINDY F. OVARD is the mother of two children and wife to the best husband on earth. She freelance writes in her spare time from being mother and wife. Cindy owns a small website designing business from her home in Southern California.

SHERRI WAAS SHUNFNTHAL is a freelance writer/poet in Northern Virginia. She has combined her love of writing, language, and poetry to form Poetry Partners – interactive poetry workshops for children up to age 90! Her essay "Pauses" currently appears in *Every Woman Has a Story* (Warner Books). Sherri's first book of poetry, *Sacred Voices: Women of Genesis Speak*, was published by Pocol Press in March 2000.

MARYBETH THAYER lives in Kerkhoven, Minnesota, just six miles from the Kelly family farm. As a staff journalist for the *Kerkhoven Banner*, she covers the activities of local and county government and writes feature stories. She has recently received two awards for her writing from the Minnesota Newspaper Association. Thayer states, "Everyone has a story to tell and it's too bad that I won't live long enough to write them all down." As a mother of four, she is routinely buried in laundry and dishes (she prefers writing to chores).

Hailing from California and a veteran of the US Air Force, DON P. WRIGHT harbored little interest in genealogy until the birth of his granddaughter in 1982. This led to his intense interest in genealogy and eventually his own newsletter and website "Footprints of Our Past." Shortly thereafter, remembering a trip he had made to Michigan to visit relatives at age eleven, Wright began to dig into his family history. He soon discovered Emma, a young child who never really knew life. That discovery created an interest that will not be forgotten.

www.ingramcontent.com/pod-product-compliance
Lightning Source LLC
Chambersburg PA
CBHW050546280326
41933CB00011B/1739